AF324649

Criminal Justice
Recent Scholarship

Edited by
Nicholas P. Lovrich

A Series from LFB Scholarly

Desistance
Ecological Factors in an Inner-City Sample

Sophie M. Aiyer

LFB Scholarly Publishing LLC
El Paso 2014

Library of Congress Cataloging-in-Publication Data

Library of Congress Cataloging-in-Publication Data

Aiyer, Sophie M., 1979-
  Desistance : ecological factors in an inner-city sample / Sophie M. Aiyer.
       pages cm. -- (Criminal justice: recent scholarship)
  Includes bibliographical references and index.
  ISBN 978-1-59332-714-9 (hardcover : alk. paper)
  1. Juvenile delinquents. 2. Criminals--Rehabilitation. 3. Deviant behavior. 4. Urban ecology (Sociology) I. Title.
  HV9069.A669 2014
  364.36--dc23
                                        2014002282

ISBN 978-1-59332-714-9

Printed on acid-free 250-year-life paper.

Manufactured in the United States of America.

Table of Contents

List of Tables

List of Figures

Acknowledgments

The study reported here was supported by funding from the Institute of Education Sciences, U.S. Department of Education, through Grant R305B040049 to the University of Virginia. The opinions expressed in this paper are those of the author, and do not represent views of the U.S. Department of Education. In addition, data analyzed were from the Chicago Youth Development Study. CYDS was funded by support from the National Institute of Mental Health (R01 48248), National Institute of Child and Health and Human Development (HS35415), Centers from Disease Control and Prevention (R49/CCR512739), and the William T. Grant Foundation.

I would like to thank those who supported me through this endeavor. First, I express thanks to my mentors, Joanna Lee Williams, Patrick Tolan, Melvin Wilson, and Xitao Fan for their thoughtful feedback and support throughout this writing process. I also give special appreciation to Joanna Lee Williams, who was an excellent mentor and to whom I am truly grateful. I express special gratitude to Patrick Tolan for providing me with guidance during this undertaking, and to Melvin Wilson, who provided me with a great deal of mentorship throughout my term as a doctoral student. Finally, I thank the Chicago Youth Development

Study investigators, for allowing me to pursue and develop my research interests with this fascinating study.

Preface

In the present study, we examined the influence of individual, family, and neighborhood factors during adolescence on desistance from antisocial behavior in early adulthood. Although a preponderance of literature exists on risk factors for the development of antisocial behavior, less is known about predicting desistance from crime. Therefore, we examined the direct, indirect, and interactive influence of ecological factors on desistance in a sample of low-income, urban males followed from early adolescence into early adulthood. Binary logistic regression techniques were used to test our hypotheses.

Results supported predictions for the roles of aggression, parental discipline, and exposure to neighborhood violence in predicting desistance. Yet, aggression became a non-significant predictor after accounting for family and neighborhood factors, suggesting the possibility that risk could be explained by additional, intervening variables. Furthermore, discipline moderated the effect of aggression on desistance in aggressive youth. Mother's antisocial behavior partially explained the effect of aggression on desistance, emphasizing the powerful role of parenting behavior. Mother's antisocial behavior also moderated the effect of discipline, indicating that disciplinary parenting no longer had a positive influence when mothers were highly antisocial. Discipline maintained significance even after neighborhood effects were accounted for, identifying parenting factors as the strongest predictors of later desistance. Collectively, our findings underscore the need to examine factors in multiple domains of a child's ecology in order to fully understand later desistance.

Chapter One
An Ecological Approach to Antisocial Behavior

Although there is a substantive body of literature on precursors and correlates of the initiation and development of antisocial behavior, less is known about factors that influence a decline in antisocial behavior during young adulthood (Monahan, Steinberg, Cauffman, & Mulvey, 2009). Moreover, research has focused on risk factors for the development and persistence of antisocial behavior more than on protective factors associated with a decreased probability of later delinquency (Lösel& Bender, 2003). However, research on desistance from crime may be best predicted by a combination of both risk and protective factors (Stouthamer-Loeber, Loeber, Stallings, & Lacourse, 2008).

Ecological theorists assert that human development and behavior evolve as a function of the interplay between the individual child and his or her social environment (Bronfenbrenner, 1979). Developmental theorists propose that although antisocial behavior may be based on biological predisposition, vulnerability is exacerbated by environmental factors over time (Moffitt, 1990; Moffitt, Caspi, Harrington, & Milne, 2002). Exposure to deleterious environments on multiple levels of a child's social ecology can exacerbate existing behavioral problems (Sameroff, 2007; Miech, Caspi, Moffitt, Wright, & Silva, 1999). Additionally, children with high vulnerability levels are influenced particularly strongly by toxic contextual influences (Luthar & Zigler, 1991). Although much research has focused on microsystem level processes as the proximal training ground for antisocial behavior, such as interactions with parents, siblings, and peers (Dishion & Patterson, 2006); less is known about broader contextual influences that predict desistance from offending.

Family processes at the microsystem level play a prominent role in determining behavioral outcomes. Low parental involvement, low family cohesiveness, and poor parent-child communication increase risk for juvenile delinquency and youth violence (Capaldi & Patterson, 1994; Gorman-Smith, Tolan, Zelli, & Huesmann, 1996). Harsh and inconsistent parental discipline is a strong predictor of antisocial behavior, along with poor parental supervision, weak parental monitoring and lack of warmth between a parent and child (Patterson, Reid, & Dishion, 1992; Dodge & Pettit, 2003). Although there have been robust findings for family factors influencing delinquency in adolescence, few studies have looked at the impact of family processes on desistance from crime. There is some evidence for the prominent role of stable marital relationships and family social bonds in predicting desistance (Sampson & Laub, 1993). Youth who desist also report higher levels of family involvement and stronger, positive relationships with family members (van Domburgh et al., 2009).

Neighborhood processes at the exosystem level also influence risk for antisocial behavior. Exposure to environmental adversity, stress, and neighborhood violence increase a child's risk for developing antisocial behavior (Lahey, Miller, Gordon, & Riley, 1999). Specifically, risk factors such as living in high-crime neighborhoods and inner-city environments, along with exposure to family disadvantage and residential crowding elevate risk for behavioral problems (Coie & Dodge, 1998). Neighborhood disorganization and weak informal social control are thought to reduce a community's ability to regulate the behavior of adolescents (Sampson, Raudenbush, & Earls, 1997); yet, research is still needed on how neighborhood factors influence pathways of antisocial behavior, and particularly the desistance process.

Early antisocial behavior strongly predicts later antisocial behavior. Yet, not all children who display early behavioral problems continue to exhibit such behavior over the life course (Moffitt, Caspi, Dickson, Silva, & Stanton, 1996). In fact, antisocial behavior is only highly stable and consistent among males with extreme behavioral problems (Caspi & Moffitt, 1992). As relatively few offenders continue offending during adulthood (Loeber & Farrington, 2000; Moffitt, 1993), this underscores the importance of identifying which risk and protective factors distinguish youth who desist from those who continue to offend.

Chronic offenders demonstrate higher levels of early disruptive behavior and experience more social disadvantage compared to their desisting counterparts (van Domburgh, Loeber, Bezemer, Stallings, & Stouthamer-

Loeber, 2009). In addition, antisocial youth who do not desist after adolescence tend to have have less inhibitory control and more family instability compared to their childhood-limited peers (Veenstra, Lindenberg, Verhulst & Ormel, 2009). Furthermore, desisters may be identified based differential exposure to protective factors including attachment to institutions and social bonds, as well as based on age of onset (Sampson & Laub, 1990). Sampson and Laub (1993) suggest that social bonds to people and institutions in both the neighborhood and family context predict desistance from crime.

RESEARCH QUESTIONS AND HYPOTHESES

Based on the previously discussed theoretical background and empirical findings, the present study examines the influence and interplay of individual, family, and neighborhood factors on desistance from antisocial behavior in late adolescence. The study is guided by the following research questions and hypotheses.

1. How do individual levels of aggression and impulsivity predict desistance from antisocial behavior?

    a. <u>Hypothesis 1a</u>. Individual characteristics (e.g., aggression and impulsivity) will be negatively associated with desistance from crime. In addition, aggression is predicted to be a stronger risk factor relative to impulsivity.

    b. <u>Hypothesis 1b.</u> Aggression will exacerbate the effect of impulsivity on desistance. Impulsivity is hypothesized to be a stronger risk factor for highly aggressive youth.

2. How do parental discipline, parental monitoring, and mother's antisocial behavior predict desistance? In addition, does parenting moderate or mediate risk from individual characteristics on desistance?

    a. <u>Hypothesis 2a</u>. Family protective factors (e.g., parental discipline and parental monitoring) will be positively associated with desistance, and mother's antisocial behavior will be negatively associated with desistance.

    b. <u>Hypothesis 2b</u>. Parental discipline will buffer the association between aggression and desistance. Discipline is hypothesized to be a stronger protective factor for highly aggressive youth in promoting desistance.

    c. <u>Hypothesis 2c</u>. Mother's antisocial behavior will mediate the association between aggression and desistance, by explaining some or all of the association between aggression and desistance.

    d. <u>Hypothesis 2d</u>. Mother's antisocial behavior is also hypothesized to mediate the association between parental discipline and desistance, by explaining some or all of the association between discipline and desistance.

3. How do neighborhood social processes, neighborhood resources, and exposure to neighborhood violence predict desistance?

    a. <u>Hypothesis 3a</u>. Neighborhood risk factors (e.g., exposure to neighborhood violence) will be negatively associated with desistance, while neighborhood protective factors (e.g., neighborhood resources and neighborhood social cohesion) will be positively associated with desistance.

    b. <u>Hypothesis 3b.</u> Exposure to violence will exacerbate the effect of aggression on desistance. Exposure to violence is hypothesized to be a stronger risk factor for highly aggressive youth.

4. Is there a significant cross-setting interaction and/or mediation between family and neighborhood factors?

    a. <u>Hypothesis 4a</u>. Exposure to neighborhood violence will moderate the association between parental discipline and desistance. The association between discipline and desistance is hypothesized to be stronger for youth exposed to low levels of neighborhood violence.

    b. <u>Hypothesis 4b.</u> Parental discipline will mediate the association between exposure to violence and desistance, by explaining some or all of the association between exposure to violence and desistance.

KEY TERMS AND VARIABLES

<u>Individual Variables</u>
Aggression. Aggression may be defined as potentially harmful intentional behavior, committed in an aroused state and subsequently perceived as aversive by the victim (Braine, 1994). There is often a distinction made between reactive and proactive aggression, and also between overt and relational aggression (Coie & Dodge, 1998). The present study focused on the role of aggression in predicting chronic delinquency, rather than focusing on aggression subtypes.

Aggression consistently predicts later delinquency, and is often considered the behavioral feature most predictive of antisocial behavior (Dodge & Pettit, 2003; Loeber & Farrington, 2000). In addition, aggression is most strongly associated with criminal behavior when part of a constellation of behavioral problems encompassing hyperactivity, inattention, and biased social information processing (Rutter et al., 1998). We still need a better understanding regarding the role of aggression in the developmental processes that lead to desistance. Elucidating the mechanisms by which early aggression is associated with later desistance is important to further our understanding of delinquency and antisocial behavior overall.

Impulsivity. Impulsivity encompasses a cluster of behaviors relating to poor inhibitory control. Impulsive behaviors include hyperactivity, poor planning abilities, low self-control, and risk-taking behaviors (Farrington & Welsh, 2007). In the present study, impulsivity refers primarily to attention problems, thus being closely related to constructs including poor concentration, and restlessness. These attention constructs have been shown to predict risk for later delinquency and criminal behavior (Bor, McGee, & Fagan, 2004), and are therefore of interest in the present study of desistance.

Antisocial Behavior. Antisocial behavior typically refers to a wide range of socially unacceptable and deviant behaviors that take on different forms during different points in the life course (Susman, 2006). Moreover, antisocial behavior describes a cluster of problem behaviors that vary over the course of development, encompassing oppositional behavior and noncompliance in early childhood, multiple forms of aggression in middle childhood, and delinquency and substance abuse in adolescence (Dishion & Patterson, 2006). Delinquency describes law-breaking behavior by children and adolescents, and criminality describes law-breaking behavior in adults (Loeber et al., 2008). In the present study, antisocial behavior refers to behaviors that incorporate delinquency, childhood externalizing behavioral problems, juvenile delinquency, and adult criminal behavior.

Desistance. Although early antisocial behavior is associated with adult criminal behavior, most antisocial children do not become antisocial adults (Moffitt, 1993). Desistance is a process that results in the termination of antisocial behavior (Laub & Sampson, 2001), most often occurring in late adolescence and early adulthood (Stouthamer-Loeber et al., 2008). Desistance is also viewed as the absence of criminal behavior over a period of time (Farrall & Calverley, 2006), and has been described as a gradual movement away from offending (Laub et al., 1998), instead of as an abrupt event.

Age-Crime Curve

Antisocial behavior declines in prevalence in the general population as age increases. Specifically, antisocial behavior tends to increase from childhood into late adolescence, and then decreases prevalence as youth enter young adulthood (Lahey et al., 2000); this trend of decreasing delinquent behavior in early adulthood is referred to as the age-crime curve (Hirschi & Gottfreson, 1983).

Family Variables

Parental Discipline and Parent-Child Conflict. Harsh discipline is often measured based on the extent to which parents physically abuse or punish their children, as well as the degree to which this discipline is consistent or inconsistent (Conger, Patterson, & Ge, 1995). Ineffective, inconsistent discipline increases risk for later delinquency (Gorman-Smith, et al., 1999; Patterson et al., 1992).

Parent-child conflict can be defined as a composite variable that encompasses ratings of hostile and rejecting parenting, verbal and physical approval, warmth, nurturance and punitiveness between the parent and child (Ingoldsby, Shaw, Winslow, Schonberg, Gilliom, & Criss, 2006). Parent-child conflict can also be obtained from evaluating the use of negative humor, complaining, conflict, rejection, and nonverbal expressions of disengagement (Ingoldsby, et al. 2006).

Although poor parental discipline and parent-child conflict can be viewed as theoretically and empirically independent, both have been shown to increase risk for delinquency and violence (Farrington, 1994; Gorman-Smith, et al., 1996). In addition, previous investigators have measured parent-child conflict based on harsh parental discipline, family interactions around discipline, or the proportion of time parents are aversive during interactions with their children (Gorman-Smith, et al., 1998; Loeber and Stouthamer-Loeber, 1986).

Parental Monitoring. Parental monitoring describes a constellation of parenting behaviors that involve attention to and surveillance of the child's activities and whereabouts (Dishion & McMahon, 1998). Parental monitoring is associated with the safety of children (Peterson, Ewigman, & Kivlahan, 1993) and the development and maintenance of antisocial behavior (Patterson & Stouthamer- Loeber, 1984). Furthermore, there is evidence that parents of delinquent youth are less aware of where their children are and of what they are doing (Farrington & Loeber, 1999), emphasizing the importance of understanding the role of monitoring on antisocial behavior.

Mother's Antisocial Behavior. Criminal offending is known to be concentrated in families and transmitted through generations (Farrington, Barnes, & Lambert, 1996). Antisocial parents also use harsh and erratic parenting skills, provide inadequate supervision, and are more likely to have conflict with their children (Rutter et al., 1998). Family contextual factors associated with delinquency may be attenuated after controlling for parental criminality (Rowe, 1994). Thus, the role of mother's antisocial behavior is important to consider when investigating the process of desistance.

<u>Neighborhood Variables</u>
Neighborhood Social Processes Neighborhood social processes are assessed based on self-reported sense of belonging, resident support, and neighborhood involvement (Sheidow, Gorman-Smith, Tolan, & Henry, 2001). Social processes encompass constructs such as *neighborliness,* which is the extent to which individuals perceive themselves as involved with and able to depend on fellow community members (Tolan, Gorman-Smith, & Henry, 2003), and *extent of neighborhood problems,* which refers to whether participants perceive graffiti, drugs, noise, abandoned buildings, vandalism, burglary, homelessness, and gangs as being problems in their communities (Tolan et al., 2003).

Neighborhood Resources In the present study, *neighborhood resources* was used to approximate the concept of *neighborhood disadvantage* from other studies. Neighborhood disadvantage can be assessed by concentration of poverty, indicated by the percentage of families below the poverty-level, the percentage of owner-occupied housing, mobility rates, and the percentage of female-headed households (Tolan et al., 2003). Furthermore, economic resources available to and used by the community have previously been used as a proxy for neighborhood disadvantage (Tolan et al., 2003).

Exposure to Neighborhood Violence Exposure to violence is assessed based on whether participants have witnessed violence or been the victim of a violent act (Sheidow et al., 2001). Perceptions of safety are assessed based on self-reported information about the extent of fear participants have in their neighborhoods, and whether such fears limit abilities to frequent different places in their communities (Sheidow et al., 2001). Exposure to neighborhood violence has been shown to significantly contribute to risk for antisocial behavior (Spano, Vazsonyi, & Bolland, 2009); yet, family processes may mediate the effects of exposure to violence on behavioral problems (Gorman- Smith, Henry, & Tolan, 2004).

SIGNIFICANCE OF THE PRESENT STUDY

The present study was conducted to examine an ecological model of desistance using longitudinal data from a high-risk, urban male sample. The study examined risk and protective factors in individual, family, and neighborhood domains over the course of adolescence that influenced desistance from antisocial behavior in young adulthood. Furthermore, we examined whether risk from aggression varied based on level of impulsivity,_ parental discipline, and exposure to violence. We also sought to delineate the role of family factors in moderating and mediating neighborhood risk during adolescence, in an effort to identify proximal and distal factors that promote desistance. In an effort to provide a more nuanced examination of direct associations found, mediation analyses were conducted to determine the role of additional explanatory variables. Altogether, the study aimed to better understand linkages between individual, family, and neighborhood factors, as they relate to desistance.

Although much research has focused on microsystem processes influencing development, as well as interactions within the mesosystem, less is known about the interactions between various ecological settings in predicting antisocial behavior, conceptualized by Bronfenbrenner (1994) as the "exosystem". Specifically there needs to be a better understanding of the exosystem, encompassing interactions between proximal and distal contexts (Rutter, 1998). Moreover, there is a dearth of research on predictors of desistance during the transition from adolescence to adulthood (Monahan et al., 2009). Therefore, research is needed to investigate specific factors that reduce risk for antisocial behavior and promote desistance from crime, focusing on how such influences differ across varied risk profiles (Guerra, Williams, Tolan, & Modecki, 2008). Identifying factors in multiple domains that predict desistance should allow researchers to improve interventions that prevent the escalation of offending. Furthermore, understanding how to predict desistance is essential in order to effectively reduce the overall prevalence of crime (van Domburgh et al., 2009).

Chapter Two

Explanations for Delinquency and Desistance

ECOLOGICAL THEORY

An ecological approach to development emphasizes the importance of understanding interactions that take place in a child's immediate settings, as well as those in broader social and environmental contexts (Bronfenbrenner, 1979, 1994). Such an approach underscores the need to examine influences from various ecological settings in order to fully understand the process of development (Bronfenbrenner. 1994). Proximal processes take place within a child's immediate environment and are therefore considered part of the microsystem (Bronfenbrenner, 1994); the family context is a microsystem of particular importance in the present study. Furthermore, the impact of family processes varies as a function of the broader environmental context and of the individual characteristics of the child (Bronfenbrenner, 1994). Distal contexts (e.g., neighborhoods) as well as proximal contexts (e.g., families), influence development both directly and indirectly (Brooks-Gunn, Duncan, & Aber, 1997). Moreover, proximal processes can buffer against distal processes; for instance, when parent-child relationships are stronger, neighborhood influences may be reduced (Brooks-Gunn et al., 1997).

DEVELOPMENTAL-ECOLOGICAL THEORY

Developmental theorists posit that manifestations of antisocial behavior emerge from successive transactions between a child and his social ecology over the course of development (Lahey, Waldman, & McBurnett, 1999). Furthermore, developmental theorists have recently emphasized the importance of moving beyond correlates and predictors of offending toward understanding trajectories of offending (Guerra et al., 2008). A central tenet of the developmental-ecological approach is that individual development is invariably influenced by qualities of settings to which youth are exposed (Szapocznik & Coatsworth, 1999); in addition, cumulative effects and interdependencies of such effects are considered. Such an approach focuses on how individual outcomes emerge within a multitude of settings, emphasizing variation in the influence of family factors as a function of the broader community setting (Henggeler & Borduin, 1990; Tolan, Guerra, & Kendall, 1995). Lastly, the developmental- ecological perspective underscores the importance of considering antisocial behavior onset, predicated on the assumption that salient risk factors vary over the course of development (Lahey, Waldman, & McBurnett, 1999).

ANTISOCIAL BEHAVIOR

Antisocial behavior refers to a range of socially unacceptable and deviant behaviors that take on different forms during different points in the life course (Susman, 2006). Antisocial behavior not only poses a large risk to the individual's psychosocial functioning, but also to their family, peers, and to the community at large (Dishion & Patterson, 2006). The etiology of antisocial behavior stems from a variety of factors in individual, family, and neighborhood domains. Developmental models for antisocial behavior suggest that although antisocial behavior is sometimes based on biological predisposition, vulnerability is exacerbated by environmental factors over he course of development (Moffitt, 2006). Moreover, distinct groups of juvenile offenders have been identified in previous studies based on etiologic differences, as well as differences in patterns of offending over time (Gardner, 2006).

THEORIES EXPLAINING ANTISOCIAL BEHAVIOR

Several developmental theoretical models seek to explain variation in the onset, continuity, and developmental progression of antisocial behavior over time. Etiologic theories differentiate groups of offenders based on individual characteristics, environmental factors, and subsequent patterns of delinquency (Loeber & Stouthamer-Loeber, 1998; Moffitt, 1993; Patterson, DeBaryshe, & Ramsey, 1989). Classifying offenders based on past and present offending behavior is based on the rationale that identifying similar groups of offenders will encourage the identification of youth at risk for persistent offending (Gardner, 2006).

Consistently, Moffitt (1993) proposes a theoretically derived classification system that identifies groups of offenders based both on etiological profiles and patterns of antisocial behavior. Specifically, Moffitt posits that there are distinct etiologies and developmental pathways that characterize juvenile offenders as either "life-course persistent" or "adolescent-limited", based on age of onset and on trajectories of behavioral problems (Moffitt, 1993). Life-course persistent offenders demonstrate early signs of behavioral problems including disinhibition, impulsivity, self-destructiveness, and deviancy; such youth are postulated to have psychological vulnerabilities that interact with dysfunctional aspects of their environments over time, culminating in chronic antisocial behavior (Moffitt, 1993; Moffitt & Caspi, 2001). Adolescent-limited offenders represent the majority of juvenile offenders; such youth typically exhibit antisocial behavior that is relatively normal and adjustive, beginning in adolescence and desisting once youth reach adulthood (Moffitt, 1993).

Additionally, Patterson et al. (1989) propose two main pathways toward criminal behavior, namely an "early starter" path and a "late starter" pathway. Specifically, coercive parenting, poor academic achievement, and early signs of aggression characterize the *early starter path*, and poor parental monitoring, oppositional behavior, and deviant peer relationships characterize the *late starter path* (Patterson et al., 1989). In addition, investigators attest that the pathway to chronic delinquency is characterized by a specific developmental sequence of experiences (Patterson et al., 1989). Such experiences begin with ineffective and coercive parenting in the family context, followed by academic failure and peer rejection in the school context, followed by a gravitation to deviant peers during early adolescence (Patterson, et al., 1989). Patterson et al.'s (1989) model emphasizes the crucial role of parents and family interactions in socializing children to be delinquent.

Other researchers have distinguished offenders based mostly on seriousness of offending, predicated on the assumption that this criterion will facilitate identifying groups with unique etiologies and patterns of offending over time (Loeber & Farrington, 1998). Loeber and Farrington (1998) assert that there are two important groups of juvenile offenders, namely *serious and violent* juveniles and *non- serious and non- violent* offenders. Likewise, there has been additional evidence to suggest that serious, violent delinquents are more likely to experience risk factors in multiple domains, compared to their non-violent counterparts (Huizinga & Jakob-Chien, 1998). Furthermore, Gorman-Smith, Tolan, Loeber, and Henry (1998) identified four distinct groups based on delinquency risk and involvement: *non-offenders, chronic minor offenders, escalators*, and *serious chronic offenders*, whose patterns of antisocial behavior are consistent with other studies on patterns of offending (Loeber et al., 1991). In addition to identifying developmental pathways of delinquency, Chicago Youth Development Study investigators also evaluated associations with patterns of family problems, demonstrating the meaningful influence of family functioning on delinquency involvement across time (Gorman- Smith et al., 1998).

Although there is support for the existence of distinct groups of delinquents, Sampson and Laub (2003) argued that the groups of offenders proposed by Moffitt (1993) actually demonstrate similar trajectories of antisocial behavior over time. Furthermore, Sampson and Laub (2003) identified six groups of offenders differing based on age-crime trajectories by following participants from childhood (age 7) to old age (age 70). Investigators identified two groups of desisters who resembled Moffitt's (1993) adolescent-limited group, and one group of chronic offenders, who resembled Moffitt's (1993) life-course persistent group. Both desister groups followed the prototypical age-crime curve (Gottfredson & Hirschi, 1990), thus engaging in little offending during childhood, followed by a sharp increase over the course of adolescence, ending with a steady decline in early adulthood. As suggested by the trajectory group names, the moderate group engaged in a higher rate of offending over a slightly longer period of time than did their classic counterparts. In addition, three additional offending groups were identified who displayed moderate to low chronic antisocial behavior across time. Although peak ages of offending varied between latent groups, all offenses declined systematically during middle adulthood regardless of variation in early risk factors (Sampson & Laub, 2003). Finally, early risk factors were not predictive of desistance; however childhood risk factors were predictive of delinquency level, confirming the importance of assessing individual characteristics when studying antisocial behavior patterns.

INDIVIDUAL FACTORS

<u>Early-Onset Antisocial Behavior</u>
From a developmental perspective, individual trajectories of antisocial behavior are postulated to change depending on when individuals participate in such behavior (Moffitt, 1993). Specifically, there is evidence that childhood antisocial behavior is strongly related to low verbal ability, hyperactivity, impulsivity, and neuropsychological problems (Jeglum-Bartusch, Lynam, Moffitt, & Silva, 1997; Moffitt, 1993; 2006). Furthermore, childhood-onset antisocial behavior is one of the strongest predictors of serious persistent offending in adulthood, controlling for other risk factors (Kazemian & Farrington, 2005; Simonoff et al., 2004). In addition, early-onset antisocial behavior has been more strongly associated with violence in early adulthood (Jeglum-Bartusch et al., 1997), and youth who exhibit early problem behaviors are also at risk for poor long-term adjustment in several domains (Campa, Bradshaw, Eckenrode, & Zielinksi, 2008). Moreover, there is evidence that a small group of young offenders is responsible for a large proportion of juvenile crime (Sampson & Laub, 2004), emphasizing the importance of understanding what distinguishes those who engage in problem behaviors early and show a stable pattern of antisocial behavior into adulthood, from those whose antisocial behavior is adolescent-limited. Adolescent-limited antisocial behavior has been shown to stem mainly from social processes (Moffitt, 1993, 2006), and has also been more strongly associated with non-violent outcomes (Jeglum-Bartusch et al., 1997).

Notably, although most persistent offenders tend to have long histories of problem behaviors, there is evidence that children who demonstrate early-onset antisocial behavior_ sometimes desist from offending (Moffitt et al., 2002). Early-onset youth who desist sometimes experience high levels of internalizing behaviors (Moffitt et al., 2002), and may show evidence of cognitive impairment in young adulthood (Raine, Moffitt, Caspi, Loeber, Stouthamer-Loeber, & Lynam, 2005). Although such young adults are labeled as desisters, they may experience chronic problem behaviors despite their termination of criminal offending (Campa et al., 2006). Ultimately, research is still limited on what specific mechanisms explain desistance from antisocial behavior in high-risk youth.

<u>Impulsivity and Aggression</u>
Impulsivity is a particularly strong individual predictor of delinquency, and is often measured as part of the construct of attention. Specifically, impulsivity is operationalized as the inability to inhibit actions or regulate behavior (Farrington, 1992). Constructs related to impulsivity include hyperactivity, restlessness, a failure to plan ahead, poor self-control, a weak ability to delay gratification, sensation-seeking, and risk-taking tendencies (Farrington & Welsh, 2007). Furthermore, inattention, hyperactivity, and impulsivity demonstrate considerable continuity with later antisocial behavior (Nagin & Tremblay, 1999; Tremblay et al., 1994), and self-regulation has been shown to improve the ability to avoid committing delinquent acts. In addition, low levels of guilt, weak empathy, self-centeredness, and fearlessness increase risk for later delinquency (Farrington & Welsh, 2007). Moreover, there is evidence that

impulsivity is a stronger risk factor for delinquency in disadvantaged neighborhoods than in lower-risk neighborhoods (Lynam et al., 2000).

Importantly, impulsive youth may be neurologically predisposed to behave in an aggressive, antisocial manner (Lynam, Moffitt, and Stouthamer- Loeber, 1993). Neurobiological research has shown that the same brain structures regulate attention, impulsivity, self-monitoring, planning, and working memory (Baumeister & Hawkins, 2001). In addition, children at risk for later antisocial behavior have been identified early based on neurological abnormalities and exhibiting poor attention and oppositional behavior (Nagin & Tremblay, 1999). There is also overlap between the biological etiology of attention problems with that of aggressive behavior, as both behaviors activate similar frontal lobe areas, temporal areas, and parietal pathways. (Davidson, Putnam, & Larson, 2000).

Although impulsivity predicts later antisocial behavior (Farrington & Welsh, 2007), there is conflicting evidence for whether this risk is distinct from aggression (Moffitt, 2006). Poor impulse control and weak suppression of aggression have both been associated with serious, persistent antisocial behavior (Mulvey, Steinberg, Piquero, Besana, Fagan, Schubert et al., 2010). Furthermore, there is evidence that overt physical aggression is more predictive of later antisocial behavior than hyperactivity (Broidy, Nagin, Tremblay, Bates, Brame, & Dodge et al., 2003); however other researchers have found that early levels of hyperactivity strongly predict both adolescent-limited and life-course persistent antisocial behavior (Moffitt, 1993, 2006). Ultimately, research is needed to determine how the impact of aggression and impulsivity differ in predicting later antisocial behavior (Rutter, 2003) as these behavioral constructs tend to aggregate in high-risk youth.

<u>Physical Aggression and Violence</u>
Developmental pathways for violent and non-violent juvenile delinquency may differ; furthermore, early levels of aggression are an important precursor of serious and violent antisocial behavior (Tolan et al., 2003). Research suggests that risk for violent antisocial behavior is highest in the most aggressive children, and that stability of aggression over time is higher in serious juvenile delinquents, compared to their "exploratory" delinquent peers (Huesmann & Eron, 1984; Loeber & Hay, 1996; Tolan et al., 2003). In a longitudinal study following participants since birth, adolescent-limited offenders were found to have elevated levels of impulsivity until they were 26 years of age; whereas their life-course persistent counterparts did not demonstrate impulsivity in young adulthood (Moffitt, 2006). However, persistent offenders were found to be significantly more aggressive, alienated, and callous in young adulthood compared to the adolescent-limited group (Moffitt, 2006).

Violent antisocial behavior is a risk factor for persistent offending. Moffitt (2006) reported that life-course persistent offenders demonstrated more physical aggression in early childhood as well as more violence after age 18. Findings from the Dunedin study also showed that persisters engaged in far more domestic violence against women and children during young adulthood, compared with their adolescent-limited counterparts (Moffitt, 1993). Moffitt et al. (2006) also reported that adolescent-limited offenders engaged primarily in property crime and substance abuse in young adulthood, although rarely in violent offending (Moffitt, 2006). Fergusson, Horwood, and Ridder (2005) confirmed the aforementioned findings, reporting that serious, violent offenders were much more likely to persist in antisocial behavior after age 25 compared with the non-violent participants.

FAMILY PROCESSES

Although youth aggression is a strong predictor of subsequent involvement in antisocial behavior, the family plays a prominent role in determining developmental outcomes. The family unit can function as a mediator of both proximal and distal risk factors on children, such as social class or economic hardship (Masten & Shaffer, 2007; Simons, 2001). Families also serve a moderating role, where family members buffer or exacerbate the effect of proximal and distal conditions on child outcomes (Masten & Shaffer, 2007). Social influences in the family context are contended to account for the continuity of antisocial behavior after childhood (Laub & Sampson, 2003; Sampson & Laub, 1990), above and beyond risk from individual predisposition.

Family functioning is influential to the development of behavioral problems, and there is evidence that antisocial behavior runs in families (Farrington et al., 1996). Familial correlates to antisocial behavior include teen parents, family poverty, and family dysfunction (Nagin & Tremblay, 1999). Harsh parental discipline, poor parental supervision, weak parental monitoring and poor parent-child relationships have been shown to mediate the association between family poverty and youth violence (Nagin & Tremblay, 1999). Furthermore, inconsistent and erratic parental discipline along with negative and rejecting parenting predict risk for antisocial behavior (Patterson, Reid, & Dishion, 1992). Low parental involvement and poor parent-child communication increase also risk for juvenile delinquency (Capaldi & Patterson, 1996), and low family cohesiveness is yet another strong predictor of youth violence (Gorman-Smith et al., 1996).

Family risk factors are consistently associated with the development and persistence of antisocial behavior, whereas family protective factors predict desistance from offending. Family involvement and positive family relationships promote desistance, specifically in high-risk males (van Domburgh et al., 2009). Moffitt (1993, 2006) suggests that the etiology of persistent antisocial behavior emerges from a neuro-developmental predisposition combined with inadequate parenting, disrupted family bonds and family poverty. In the Dunedin study, the persistent pathway was unequivocally associated with early parenting risk factors including harsh and inconsistent discipline, family conflict, low family socioeconomic status and maternal neglect; in contrast, men who desisted had family backgrounds that were considered relatively normative (Moffit & Caspi, 2001; Moffitt, 2006). Also, family background in the Dunedin study was measured with indicators including teen motherhood, social class, family conflict, number of caretaker changes, years living with a single mother, harsh and inconsistent parental discipline, and poor parent-child relationship quality (Jaffee, Caspi, Moffitt, Taylor, & Dickson, 2001).

<u>Parenting</u>
Parenting practices are defined as parenting strategies used to gain children's compliance, maintain control, and enforce expectations (Darling & Steinberg, 1993). Parenting practices are thought to have a direct effect on developmental outcomes, while parenting style refers to characteristics that moderate the effectiveness of practices (Darling & Steinberg, 1993). Therefore, parenting style is conceptualized as a context that moderates the impact of parenting practices on child outcomes (Darling & Steinberg, 1993). Parenting style should ideally be distinguished from parenting practices to better understand processes underlying developmental socialization (Darling & Steinberg, 1993).

Furthermore, parenting styles typically describe parent's actions; however, parent-child interactions are thought to mediate the association between parenting styles and behavioral outcomes (Collins & Madsen, 2002). Parenting style traditionally refers to dimensions of punitiveness (e.g., physical discipline or restrictions of activities) and permissiveness (e.g., tolerance for child transgressions) as responses to child aggression (Sears, Maccoby, & Levin, 1957). Furthermore, parenting styles are defined as attitudes and emotional stances that impact parent-child relationship quality (Baumrind, 1991). Finally, parental control, monitoring, and discipline are key components of parenting style (Baumrind, 1991).

<u>Parent- Child Conflict</u>
Parent-child conflict refers to the quality of the parent-child relationship and is commonly indexed by negative parenting behavior, abusive parenting, and erratic discipline

skills (Dishion, Capaldi, & Yoerger, 1999). In addition, conflict clusters with constructs of negativity, irritability, and low levels of warmth and control (Amato, 2001).Parent-child conflict has been identified as a robust predictor of early aggression and adolescent antisocial behavior (Patterson et al., 1992). Consistently, there is evidence for a direct link between parent-child conflict and behavioral problems in early to middle childhood (Shaw, Criss, Schonberg, & Beck, 2004). Furthermore, parent-child conflict has been shown to mediate the association between family poverty and adolescent delinquency (Wadsworth & Compass, 2002). In addition, relationship conflict may continue for youth who demonstrate high aggression in early childhood, serving to reinforce and escalate antisocial behavior across adolescence (Gorman-Smith, Tolan, & Henry, 2000; Shaw et al., 2004). Correspondingly, parent-child coercion and parental disengagement contribute to the developmental course of aggression (Hart, Nelson, Robinson, Olsen, & McNeilly-Choque). In addition, family dysfunction and poor parent-child relationships have been shown to predict higher levels of aggression (Bornstein & Cote, 2006), and hostile parenting explains risk from early aggression on later aggression (Bornstein & Cote, 2006).

<u>Conflict and Discipline</u>
Parent-child conflict can be operationalized using measures that assess the manner in which parents discipline their children (Earls, Brooks-Gunn, Raudenbush, & Sampson, 2002). Harsh parenting is thought to contribute to higher levels of child externalizing behavior by promoting norms supportive of aggression and violence (Catalano &

Hawkins, 1996). In addition, social learning theorists suggest that the association between poor parenting practices and delinquency can be explained by behavioral modeling across generations (Patterson, 1995). There is also evidence that the association between harsh parenting and aggression is mediated by both parental emotionality and child emotional regulation (Chang, Schwartz, Dodge, McBride- Chang, 2003; Deater-Deckard & Dodge, 1997).

<u>Discipline Practices</u>
Harsh, erratic and inconsistent discipline during childhood, along with negative and rejecting parenting elevate risk for later antisocial behavior, delinquency, and violence (Dodge, Bates, & Pettit, 1990; Gardner, Shaw, Dishion, Burton, & Supplee, 2007; Patterson, et al., 1992). Furthermore, low levels of parent-child warmth also increase risk for the development of antisocial behavior (Dodge & Pettit, 2003). Punitive discipline during childhood has also been strongly associated with violent arrests, domestic violence and child maltreatment in young adulthood (Eron et al., 1991).

Discipline practices can be considered positive based on how effective the parenting is in controlling the child's behavior (Tolan et al., 2003). Positive discipline can be assessed based on parents' consistent use of verbal encouragement and reinforcement in response to children's positive behaviors (Webster-Stratton, 1998). Avoidant discipline is characterized by a reluctance to discipline and provide consequences to the child, based on fear of resulting escalation of aggression and coercive behavior (Tolan et al., 2003). Positive discipline practices have been said to prevent behavior problems and promote positive outcomes (Sears & Sears, 1995).

Normative discipline styles tend to vary by race and ethnic group, suggesting that discipline might have a qualitatively different meaning based on the broader cultural context. African American parents report using more physical discipline compared with Caucasian parents (Farrington, Loeber, & Stouthamer-Loeber, 2003); however, the subtle meaning of such behaviors interpreted by the child may differ based on the presence of other parenting dimensions. Although physical discipline increases risk for aggression, maternal emotional support has been shown to moderate this association (McLoyd, 1998). Similarly, the association between harsh punishment and poor cognitive outcomes has been buffered by high maternal warmth in at-risk children (Smith & Brooks-Gunn, 1997). Furthermore, the impact of discipline may differ based on the broader community context in which the discipline takes place. For example, because low-income, ethnic minority families are more likely to live in dangerous neighborhoods, punitive parenting may not be as harmful as for youth living in neighborhoods with more resources and less violence (Furstenberg, Cook, Eccles, Elder & Sameroff, 1999).

<u>Parental monitoring</u>
Poor parental supervision and weak parental monitoring are consistently associated with the development of antisocial behavior (Patterson et al., 1992; Nagin & Tremblay, 1999; Dodge & Pettit, 2003). Parents who exhibit poor behavioral management skills and weak parental supervision may increase their children's risk for engaging in delinquency (Patterson et al., 1992). Effective parental monitoring refers to parents' knowledge of their children's whereabouts and

activities (Kerr & Stattin, 2000). Importantly, ineffective parental monitoring during childhood has been shown to predict subsequent delinquent behavior, even after controlling for early behavioral problems (Pettit, Bates, Dodge, & Meece, 1999).

Active parental monitoring and supervision are presumed to serve a critical function by altering a child's exposure to other influential social contexts in the microsystem (Dodge & Pettit, 2003). Law and Barber (2007) found that adolescents with higher levels of parental monitoring and lower levels of parental psychological control had lower risk for antisocial behavior. Furthermore, high levels of parental knowledge have been linked to positive adjustment in children, even after the impact of other parental attributes (e.g., harsh discipline) was controlled for (Lansford, Chang, Dodge, Malone, Oburu, & Palmerus et al., 2005).

Research indicates that low-income parents are more likely to use a punitive parenting style and less likely to provide support to their children compared with middle-class parents (McLoyd, 1990). Moreover, punitive parenting is associated with risk for abuse and neglect, which are parenting behaviors that may be more prevalent in low-income families (Azar, 2002). Finally, research on impoverished families emphasizes the need for more empirical work on how structural characteristics influence both parenting styles and practices that subsequently impact child development.

<u>Antisocial Parents</u>
Antisocial parents have been identified as a strong predictor of youth violence and offending in young adulthood

(Lipsey & Derzon, 1998). Additionally, criminal offending typically runs in families (Farrington, Jolliffe, Loeber, Stouthamer-Loeber, & Kalb, 2001). Although family history of antisocial behavior is recognized as a risk factor for delinquency, it is often overlooked in studies focusing on the environmental transmission of antisocial behavior.

Antisocial behavior may be transmitted from parents to their children for a multitude of reasons. It is possible that such families are characterized by a constellation of risk factors including living in disadvantaged neighborhoods, experiencing high family conflict, and being faced with family poverty, thus collectively contributing to youth's risk for delinquency and violence (Farrington & Welsh, 2007). Therefore, youth with antisocial parents may simply be exposed to more cumulative environmental risk factors than their normative counterparts. Based on such an explanation, the intergenerational transmission of antisocial behavior is one component of a larger cycle between deprivation and crime (Farrington & Welsh, 2007)

On the other hand, it is possible that parent criminality impacts youth antisocial behavior through other environmental mechanisms, subsequently being mediated by poor parental supervision, large family size, and low emotional attachment (Sampson & Laub, 1993). Consistently, antisocial parents may be less likely to provide adequate supervision and may be more likely to exhibit poor child rearing practices characterized by harsh and inconsistent discipline (Rutter, 1997). Therefore, observable aspects of the family environment may be influenced by a parent's genetic predisposition (Rutter, 1997). Consistently, parent criminality has been shown to have an attenuated effect on youth antisocial behavior when other family factors are accounted for, and vice versa (Rutter, 1997).

Finally, another explanation for the transmission of antisocial behavior is that the influence of parental criminality is mediated by genetic mechanisms, thus representing a gene-environment interaction (Raine, 1993). Therefore, poor parenting might be a stronger risk factor in youth with antisocial parents, because of the presence of both genetic and environmental risk in such families (Rutter, 1998). In other words, it is possible that the effect of family risk factors is greater for children with a genetic predisposition for antisocial behavior. Moreover, mother's antisocial behavior could exert a deleterious influence on youth because of genetic factors, environmental factors, or both. Although it was not possible to decipher whether the transmission of antisocial behavior was based on genetic or environmental explanations in the present study, the direct and indirect impact of mother's antisocial behavior was examined.

NEIGHBORHOOD INFLUENCES

Recognizing that children are influenced by factors in multiple settings of their social ecology is essential to understanding the processes through which families and neighborhoods influence children (Sameroff, 2007). Environmental factors that elevate risk for developing conduct problems include poverty, crowding, inner-city environments, and unemployment (Coie & Dodge, 1998). Consistently, previous studies have shown that both adolescent delinquency and crime are most prevalent within neighborhood contexts characterized by disadvantage, population density, and low organizational participation (Sampson & Groves, 1989; Leventhal & Brooks-Gunn, 2000). Furthermore, there is a strong, consistent link between exposure to community violence and subsequent psychological adjustment; however, not all children who are exposed to violence develop antisocial behavior (Luthar & Goldstein, 2004). Although neighborhoods often influence youth outcomes through family risk factors, neighborhood deprivation also influences development in ways that are independent of family- deprivation (Coie & Dodge, 1998; Duncan, Brooks-Gunn, & Klebanov, 1994).

Neighborhood and community influences beyond the family tend to become increasingly influential during adolescence, as adolescence represents a critical stage during which youth have gained independence and autonomy from parents, and are often less carefully supervised and monitored by adults (Steinberg & Morris, 2001; Dishion & McMahon, 1998). Consequently, children who are raised in low-income, inner-city neighborhoods may be at greater risk for chronic delinquency compared to those raised in lower-risk contexts (Wikstrom & Loeber, 1999), emphasizing the importance of studying the impact of neighborhood processes as children mature.

Neighborhood Disadvantage and Resources
Neighborhood disadvantage and structural poverty are associated with elevated risk for adolescent delinquency and adult criminal offending. Adolescent antisocial behavior is significantly more prevalent in low-income neighborhoods (Sampson et al., 1997), and exposure to persistent poverty across childhood predicts later

behavioral problems (Guerra, Huesmann, Tolan, Van Acker, & Eron, 1995). In addition, the association between community poverty and antisocial behavior is strongest when examining pathways to serious violent delinquency, and when adolescents experience poverty during early childhood and over prolonged periods of time (McLoyd, Kaplan, Purtell, Bagley, Hardaway, & Smalls, 2009). Furthermore, concentrated disadvantage, immigrant status, and residential stability are differentially associated with homicide rates in disadvantaged neighborhoods (Morenoff, Sampson, & Raudenbush, 2001). In addition, spatial proximity to risk coupled with low social and economic capacity increase risk for urban violence (Morenoff, et al., 2001; Sampson et al., 1997). Altogether, economic deprivation is one of the most influential neighborhood risk factors for delinquency (Chung & Steinberg, 2006; Hawkins, Arthur, & Catalano, 1995).

Moreover, economic inequalities and associated patterns of community instability and racial segregation can deprive communities of resources essential to promote healthy child development (Krivo & Peterson, 1996; Jencks & Mayer, 1990; Wilson, 1996). Resources are a fundamental mechanism through which neighborhoods influence behavioral outcomes (Sampson, Morenoff, & Gannon- Rowley, 2002), and describe institutions that address the needs of community residents (Sampson et al., 1997). Invariably, low-income neighborhoods typically lack important resources essential to promoting positive development, including recreational facilities, childcare centers, grocery stores, and pharmacies (Wilson, 1987, 1996).

Neighborhood Social Processes

Social capital, social cohesion, collective efficacy, and routine activities are critical mechanisms through which neighborhoods influence behavior (Sampson et al., 2002). Social capital refers to the presence of social ties and the quality of social interactions;_ social cohesion refers to the presence of strong social bonds; collective efficacy refers to the presence of mutual trust and informal social control; and routine activities refer to the ways in which the location of places promote and facilitate positive and negative actions (Sampson et al., 1997). In addition, the association between social ties, social networks, and crime operates across racial and ethnic groups in low-income areas (Sampson et al., 1997), demonstrating the importance of social cohesion in explaining urban violence. According to social disorganization theories, associations between neighborhood risk and antisocial behavior result from the ineffective social control mechanisms and weak social bonds that characterize low-income, urban areas (Sampson & Groves, 1989).

Both structural characteristics and social aspects of neighborhoods have been shown to influence the development and maintenance of antisocial behavior over time (Sampson et al., 1997; Sampson, Morenoff, & Earls, 1999; Browning, Burrington, Leventhal, & Brooks-Gunn, 2008). Neighborhoods characterized by economic decline, instability, tension between residents, and limited resources are hypothesized to have low levels of collective efficacy thus facilitating crime and antisocial behavior (Sampson et al., 1997). Furthermore, neighborhood social processes have been shown to mediate the impact of community structural characteristics on youth violence (Browning et al., 2008; Sampson et al., 1997). Social processes include perceived social support and cohesion, sense of community belonging, supervision and monitoring of children by adults, and organizational participation (Sampson et al., 1999).

Social ties and social control have been shown to decrease risk for criminal and deviant behavior (Sampson & Laub, 1993). Social investment and social capital in relationships, whether involving family, work, or the community, are proposed to influence the salience of social control (Farrall & Calverley, 2007). Furthermore, lack of social capital is thought to be a primary feature of weak social bonds (Coleman, 1990), emphasizing the importance of identifying individual and contextual factors that facilitate social control, in order to reduce risk for stable antisocial behavior.

Neighborhood Crime and Violence

Urban youth are at higher risk for exposure to community violence (Buka et al., 2001) and adolescent males tend to be exposed to particularly high rates of violence compared to other population subgroups (Gorman-Smith & Tolan, 1998). In addition, exposure to neighborhood violence is associated with aggression, violent behavior, and patterns of escalating offending (Gorman-Smith & Tolan, 1998; Gorman-Smith et al., 2000; Gorman- Smith et al., 2004). Perceptions of neighborhood danger have been associated with positive beliefs about aggressive behavior, as well as with weapon carrying and fighting (Colder et al., 2000). Although community violence is highly prevalent in inner-city neighborhoods, not all youth who are exposed to violence develop serious antisocial behavior (Tolan &

Henry, 1996), emphasizing the importance of studying the impact of exposure to violence on the desistance process.

NEIGHBORHOOD INFLUENCES MEDIATED BY FAMILIES

Ecological theorists contend that the exosystem encompasses interactions between proximal and distal contexts of the child (Bronfenbrenner, 1979). As previously discussed, distal factors encompassing neighborhood disadvantage, social cohesion, and exposure to violence, all contribute to antisocial behavior. However, a critical question is whether such distal factors influence behavioral problems directly or indirectly. This question is particularly important considering the existing evidence suggesting that neighborhoods impact youth directly, and indirectly through their effects on family processes (Jaffee et al., 2007; Gottfredson, McNeil,& Gottfredson, 1991). In addition, Sampson and Laub (1997) reported that harsh discipline, low supervision, and weak parent-child relationships explained a significant amount of the association between poverty and juvenile delinquency. Investigators consistently found that family processes mediated approximately seventy-five percent of the effect of structural background characteristics on adolescent delinquency (Sampson & Laub, 1993), affirming the purpose of considering the family when seeking to understand processes operating in the broader structural context. Furthermore, the family may be a primary explanatory mechanism for why not all children who live in high poverty neighborhoods exhibit violent behavior (Spano et al., 2009).

Neighborhood disadvantage has been shown to manifest itself through family dysfunction, poor parenting, and maternal depression (Kohen, Leventhal, Dahinten, & McIntosh, 2008). Correspondingly, problematic parenting has been shown to mediate the effect of low socioeconomic status, residential instability, and unemployment on behavioral problems in youth (Masten & Shaffer, 2007). Consistently, McLoyd (1990) demonstrated that parent-child conflict accounted for the association between neighborhood poverty and aggressive behavior; a proposed explanation for this mediation is that poverty negatively impacts family stress and disorganization, simultaneously lowering access to resources (McLoyd, 1990). Furthermore, neighborhood deprivation has been proposed to increase children's behavioral problems by increasing parental stress, reducing available social support, and reducing access to mental health services (Sampson, 1992).

Developmental- ecological theorists propose that proximal family factors are influenced by broader community characteristics in which children and their families reside (Gorman-Smith et al., 2000; Tolan & Gorman-Smith, 1997). Tolan et al. (2003) reported a direct positive association between neighborhood risk and parental control, and subsequently suggested that in disadvantaged communities, parents may be more vigilant because they feel compelled to protect their children from community risk. Consistently, Rankin and Quane (2000) suggested that parents residing in low-income areas exert high levels of control and monitoring in an effort to protect youth from risks associated with neighborhoods danger. Therefore, restrictive parenting in high-risk communities may be a crucial mechanism in buffering youth from deleterious effects of violence exposure (Simons, Simons, Burt, Brody, & Cutrona, 2005; Wallen & Rubin, 1997). Correspondingly, parental monitoring was shown to mediate the association between exposure to violence and antisocial behavior in high-crime, disadvantaged neighborhoods (Garbarino, Kostelny, & Dubrow, 1991; Simons et al., 2005), and may also be a particularly salient protective factor for deviant youth (Pettit et al., 1999). Finally, associations between family variables and delinquency may be more pronounced in high-risk neighborhoods because there are fewer controls to prevent delinquent behavior and more opportunities to engage in crime (Sampson et al., 1997). As parenting is likely to mediate the association between broader contextual risk and antisocial behavior (McLoyd, 1990), this was important to investigate in the present study.

DESISTANCE

There is a strong association between age and crime, whereby delinquency tends to emerge in early adolescence, peak in mid- adolescence, and subsequently decrease in early adulthood (Tremblay et al., 2004). The age-crime curve has been observed across crime categories, across countries and across historical periods (Hirschi & Gottfredson, 1983). Desistance is defined as the underlying process resulting in the termination of antisocial behavior and criminal activity (Laub & Sampson, 2001). Persistence typically refers to continuous antisocial behavior that remains stable from childhood through adulthood (Sampson & Laub, 2003). Desistance is unusual to study because it is the sustained absence of an event, instead of an event that happens (Maruna, 1998). The process is likely to result from a range of complex developmental, psychological, and sociological processes (Laub & Sampson, 2001). Although most delinquent youth eventually desist from delinquency, the process is not yet well understood (Laub & Sampson, 2001).

Research on early predictors of desistance has been inconclusive. Some studies report that youth who desist from crime exhibit the same amount of early risk factors as those who continue to offend (Moffitt et al., 2002; Raine et al., 2005; Sampson & Laub, 2003). There is also evidence that childhood-onset offenders who desist exhibit high levels of internalizing disorders during young adulthood, as well as other adjustment problems (Moffitt et al., 2002; Raine et al., 2005); although other studies have shown no association between desistance and internalizing problems (van Domburgh et al., 2009). Furthermore, experiences with school dropout, incarceration, and teen pregnancy are associated with persistent offending in adulthood (Moffitt, 1993, 2006). Importantly, self-efficacy has been shown to promote the desistance process (Laub & Sampson, 2001); self-control is another characteristic that has been linked to reductions in criminal offending (Monahan et al., 2009). Desistance has also been associated with the aging process, natural maturation, and stable employment in adulthood (Laub & Sampson, 2001; Moffitt, 1993; Sampson & Laub, 1993).

Although some suggest that desistance is significantly less common among early-onset_ offenders and is mainly related to individual characteristics (Moffitt, 1993), others contend that family relationships and social bonds are salient predictors of desistance (Laub & Sampson,

2001).Sampson and Laub (1993) propose a theory of age-graded social control that emphasizes the importance of social bonds and connections between the individual and society. The social control theory suggests that the association between early delinquency and adult criminal behavior is explained by both individual characteristics and social bonds formed over time (Laub & Sampson, 2001). Moreover, risk for criminal offending is predicted to be higher when bonds and emotional attachments are weak (Laub & Sampson, 2001). Social investment in institutional relationships that involve the family, work, and the community are proposed to reduce deviant behavior over the life course; therefore, the presence of social capital increases the likelihood of desisting (Sampson & Laub, 1993). Consequently, informal social bonds are hypothesized to explain variation in criminal behavior that cannot be explained by differences in antisocial propensity (Laub & Sampson, 1993).

There is additional evidence for the meaningful role of social capital and familial social bonds in promoting desistance. Specifically, socially structured relationships in family contexts are thought to facilitate social action by generating a sense of obligation (Hagan & McCarthy, 1997). Furthermore, social capital derived from family connections has been proposed to enhance the likelihood of desistance (Farrall & Calverley, 2006). Consistently, positive marital relationships, family social ties, involvement in family activities, and small family size have been linked to a precipitous decline in offending (Laub & Sampson, 2001; Sampson & Laub, 1993; van Domburgh et al., 2009). In addition, low parental stress, good parental supervision, and high quality housing have been linked to desistance; in contrast, poor parenting practices, family conflict and family disadvantage have been linked to chronic offending (Stouthamer- Loeber et al., 2008).

Group processes and structural determinants in the neighborhood context must also be considered in order to understand the desistance process (Laub & Sampson, 2001). Interactive processes between neighborhood factors and individual characteristics predict decreased offending (Moffitt, 1997); however, the specific manner by which neighborhoods influence desistance is not yet understood (Laub & Sampson, 2001). Moreover, neighborhood gangs facilitate continual engagement in delinquent behavior, and there is evidence that gang membership typically continues into adulthood (Spergel, 1990). However, research is still needed on the role of criminal organizations and neighborhood influences on the course of delinquency (Laub & Sampson, 2001).

WEAKNESSES IN THE EXISTING LITERATURE

Several gaps in our existing knowledge about desistance from antisocial behavior remain. Empirical work is needed to improve our understanding about the impact of proximal and distal factors on delinquency, as well as interactive processes between neighborhood and family settings. Moreover, developmental research on the influence of ecological risk factors has demonstrated evidence that family processes adjust in response to the broader environmental context (Gorman-Smith, Tolan, & Henry, 2000; Tolan et al., 2003), emphasizing the importance of investigating cross-context interactions in the present study. Ultimately, there is a lack of existing research on mediators and moderators of causal processes that predict antisocial behavior (Rutter, 2003), affirming the need to identify specific environmental that exacerbate and buffer individual risk for chronic antisocial behavior.

There has been a traditional focus in the literature on negative outcomes associated with early-onset antisocial behavior, instead of on positive processes influencing the transition out of offending. However, all criminal offenders desist at some point during the life course (Sampson & Laub, 2003), affirming the importance of determining whether predictors of desistance are similar to those of delinquency initiation or whether such mechanisms are unique. Thus, the present study aims to further our knowledge about processes that promote desistance in order to create effective prevention and interventions strategies for antisocial youth.

Chapter Three

Testing Predictors of Desistance

PARTICIPANTS

The present study used data from the Chicago Youth Development Study (CYDS), an ongoing longitudinal study of the development of serious delinquent behavior among a sample of inner-city male adolescents (Tolan, 1990). Participants were initially recruited from the fifth and seventh grades of seventeen Chicago public schools. After obtaining parental permission, 1,105 boys were screened for behavior problems using the Achenbach Teacher Rating Form (TRF; Achenbach, 1991). These boys represented ninety-two percent of the population of fifth and seventh-grade boys in the participating schools. Boys were subsequently selected for participation in CYDS so that fifty percent were identified as "high risk" for the development of serious antisocial behavior based on their Teacher Rating Form Aggression Scale scores; such scores indicated that they were already engaging in high levels of aggressive behavior at Baseline (T> 70, 98th percentile). Following this categorization, participants were randomly selected from the remainder of those screened and seventy-five percent of the eligible participants completed interviews during the first wave of data collection (n= 341) (Gorman-Smith, et al., 1998).

CYDS participants consisted of boys from economically disadvantaged inner-city neighborhoods in Chicago. Sixty-three percent of participants were from single parent homes. Fifty-seven percent of participants were African American and forty-three percent were Latino. Forty-eight percent came from families with a total family income of under $10,000 per year, and seventy-four percent had a total family income of under $20,000 per year. Participants were between the ages of 10 and 15 years (mean age of 12.3 years (SD 1.3) during the first wave of interviews. In addition, mother's education was measured with a score between 1-7, ranging from 8[th]grade or less to trade or vocational school, respectively. The mean mother's education score for the whole sample was 4.03 (SD 1.52), indicating that on average, mother's reported that they had obtained "some college" education. In addition, the mean age of boys was 19.1 during the sixth wave of interviews. Seven waves of data were collected over a 15-year period (1990-2005).

PROCEDURE

Study Participants were interviewed in their homes or in a mutually agreed upon location by trained interviewers. Families participated in a joint structured problem-solving interaction task that was videotaped and coded at a later time. Following the family interaction task, individual interviews were conducted separately with the target boy and his caregiver(s). Questions covered individual (e.g., stress, coping, depression, future expectations, beliefs, delinquent behavior), family (e.g., cohesion, support, communication, discipline practices, supervision, involvement), peer (e.g., popularity, social support, delinquency), school (e.g., attitudes, achievement), and neighborhood (e.g., safety, belonging, involvement) domains. The same information was collected across informants at each wave. Total interview time at each wave was between three and three and a-half hours.

ANALYTIC SAMPLE

The CYDS research team used data from the *Self Report of Delinquency* (Elliot, Dunford, & Huizinga, 1987) and composite scores from the externalizing subscales of the *Child Behavior Checklist* (Achenbach, 1991) to classify participants into four trajectories that described patterns of offending over time: "non offenders", "chronic minor offenders", "escalating offenders", and "serious chronic and violent offenders" (Gorman-Smith, Tolan, Loeber, & Henry, 1998). Trajectories were identified using cluster analysis techniques using scores on aggression, violence, minor antisocial behavior, and serious antisocial behavior over waves 1-4. Across waves 1-4, *non offenders* displayed little to no aggression (e.g., bullying, fighting); *chronic minor offenders* displayed minor antisocial acts and aggression at every wave, but no serious delinquency or violence; *escalating offenders* displayed less delinquent acts at earlier waves with escalation to violence and/ or serious antisocial behavior during later waves (e.g., waves 3 and 4); and *serious chronic and violent offenders* displayed high levels of serious antisocial behavior and increasing violence across all four waves (Gorman-Smith et al., 1998).

The present study included 196 of the 262 CYDS participants for which there was data for waves 1-6: *chronic minor offenders* (34%, *n*= 89), *escalating offenders* (13.4%, *n* = 35), and *serious chronic and violent offenders* (27.5%, *n* = 72). *Non- offenders* (25.2%, *n*= 66) displayed no aggression or minimal aggression at baseline and no delinquent behavior or minimal delinquent behavior across all waves; therefore, this group was omitted from the analytic sample. Descriptive statistics for key study variables are presented in Table 3. As desistance is defined as the sustained absence of criminal offending (Maruna, 1998), it was substantively important to exclude the *non offenders* in order to focus on participants who engaged in some delinquent behavior during the longitudinal study. Analyzing data from the remaining three delinquency clusters facilitated an investigation of what factors distinguished participants who desisted from crime from those who continued to offend. In conclusion, the exclusion of *non-offenders* decreased the statistical power of the analyses, however narrowing the sample was necessary to maintain the theoretical conceptualization of desistance. Participants included in the analytic sample were between 10 and 15 years during wave 1 (mean age of 12.5 years(SD 1.2). In addition, mother's education for the analytic sample had a mean of 3.97 (SD 1.38), which was only slightly lower than that of the entire CYDS sample. In addition, the mean age of boys in the analytic sample was 19.6 (SD 1.4) during the sixth wave of interviews

As shown in Tables 1 and 2, descriptive statistics for key demographic variables are presented for the non-offending participants who were excluded from the present study, followed by descriptive statistics for the remaining three offender groups. The non- offenders were shown to be slightly younger than their delinquent counterparts in wave 1, and also had mother's with slightly more education overall. As mother's education is frequently associated with risk for delinquency, such a trend is to be expected.

Table 1. Descriptive Statistics for Demographic Variables: Non-Offenders

Variable	N	Range	Min	Max	Mean (SD)
Age	60	5.0	10.0	15.0	12.22 (1.06)
Ethnic Group	58	4.0	1.0	5.0	1.34 (.66)
Mother's Education	59	6.0	1.0	7.0	4.14 (1.22)
Valid *N*	50				

Note. Descriptive statistics were measured at wave 1 of data collection.

Table 2. Descriptive Statistics for Demographic Variables: Chronic Minor Offenders, Escalators, and Serious Chronic, Violent Offenders

Variable	N	Range	Min	Max	Mean (SD)
Age	166	5.0	10.0	15.0	12.51 (1.18)
Ethnic Group	190	7.0	1.0	8.0	1.49 (.89)
Mother's Education	168	6.0	1.0	7.0	3.97 (1.38)
Valid *N*	153				

Note. Descriptive statistics were measured at wave 1 of data collection.

Lastly, listwise deletion was the method used to handle missing data in the present study, thus leaving participants with complete data available. Although the listwise deletion method inevitably decreases statistical power, there are issues with introducing biased estimates of missing coefficients when imputing data (Allison, 2001). In addition, almost all missing data in the present study was in the desistance outcome variable, measured across two waves of data. Furthermore, imputing missing outcome data can introduce bias, particularly when outcomes are being measured across more than one time point (Sterne, White, Carlin, Spratt, Kenward, Wood & Carpenter, 2009). Therefore, missing data was deleted in the present study, despite the corresponding decrease in sample size.

MEASURES

A description of the measurement instruments used to construct key variables are presented in the following section. The specific constructs calculated for the present study are presented below their corresponding measures. Constructs are organized by the domain they represent; specifically, constructs represent individual, family, and neighborhood domains.

ANALYTIC CONSTRUCTS

<u>Individual Measures and Constructs</u>
Self-Report Delinquency (Elliot et al., 1987). The *SRD* for CYDS was developed based on measures designed and used by Elliot, Loeber, et al. (Elliot et al., 1987; Loeber, Wung, Keenan, Giroux, Stouthamer- Loeber, Van Kammen,

& Maughan, 1993). Participants were questioned about frequency of involvement in thirty-eight criminal acts (including drug and alcohol use) using the modified self-report of delinquency (Elliot et al., 1987). The CYDS *SRD* measure assesses both the type and amount of antisocial, delinquent, and violent behavior engaged in by participants (Gorman-Smith, Tolan, & Henry, 1999).

Offenses committed by participants are classified into eight categories based on legal criteria. The categories include (1) status offenses, (2) class C misdemeanors, (3) class B misdemeanors, (4) class A misdemeanors, (5) class 4 felonies, (6) class 3 felonies, (7) class 2 felonies, and (8) class 1 felonies. Offenses are ranked in order of severity as listed above, with status offenses being the least serious and class 1 felonies being the most serious. From such a classification, estimated legal severity of offenses committed may be measured through statistical analyses. Furthermore, several items of the *SRD* can be combined to measure level of "street violence" the participant engaged in (e.g., whether the participant has attached someone with a weapon, hit someone with the intent to hurt, engaged in gang fights, etc.) (Tolan, Gorman-Smith, & Henry, 2002).

Desistance. Using previously calculated scores from the *CYDS Self-Report Delinquency Measure* (Elliot et al., 1987; Tolan et al., 2002), participants were assigned a "delinquency" score representing the sum of the frequency of each delinquent act multiplied by its weight based on legal seriousness (Tolan et al., 2002). Scores ranged from 0 to 4 with higher scores representing a high frequency of violent behavior as well as a high level of seriousness of delinquent acts. Participants are asked about their engagement in delinquent behavior during the last year. In the present study, delinquency scores from waves 5 and 6 (corresponding to ages 16-22) were used to assess desistance from antisocial behavior in late adolescence and young adulthood. *Desistance* was defined as minimal to no engagement in antisocial behavior in both waves 5 and 6. Specifically, participants who received a score of 0 in both waves were labeled as *desisters* and given a score of 1.Participants who received a score between 1-4 were labeled as *persisters* and given a score of 0. Operationalizing desistance as a dichotomous variable preserved the definition of desistance as the absence of antisocial behavior, instead of defining it as relatively less participation in antisocial behavior.

*Child Behavior Checklist for Ages 4-18 (*CBCL/4-18; Achenbach, 1991). The *CBCL* is a measure given to parents to assess children's competencies, as well to assess emotional and behavior problems. The *CBCL* is comprised of eight subscales that measure social withdrawal, somatic complaints, anxiety and depression, social problems, thought problems, attention problems, delinquent behavior, and aggressive behavior. From each of these eight subscales, it yields both broad and narrow- band factors of internalizing and externalizing problems normalized within gender and age groups. The *CBCL* has been adapted as a self-report for adolescents, named the *Youth Self Report (YSR)*. The items from the *YSR* are parallel to the items from the *CBCL*, although some items have been deleted, added, or changed to make it more appropriate for children's self reports of their competencies and problems (Tolan, Gorman-Smith, & Henry, 2001).

In both the *CBCL* and *YSR*, respondents must respond on a 3-point Likert scale of how much each item describes the youth's behavior (0 = not true about youth, 1 =somewhat or sometimes true about youth, 2 = very true or often true). Scores on each subscale are computed by averaging the scores across all subscale items. Higher scores indicate a greater degree of emotional and behavioral problems (Tolan, Gorman-Smith, & Henry, 2001b).

Aggression and Impulsivity Externalizing subscale scores from waves 1-4 of the parent and child reports of the *CBCL* were aggregated to assess *aggression* and *impulsivity.* Specifically, *aggressive behavior* and *delinquent behavior* subscale scores were used to estimate *aggression*, and *attention problem* subscale scores were used to assess *impulsivity.* Items assessing attention include questions such as "You have trouble concentrating or paying attention"; items assessing aggression include questions such as "You argue a lot", and items assessing delinquency include questions such as "You physically attack people". Cronbach's alpha was 0.80 for the *attention problems* subscale, 0.91 for the *aggressive behavior* subscale, and 0.77 for the *delinquent behavior* subscale (all assessed at wave 2) (Tolan et al., 2001b).

Family Measures and Constructs
Parenting Practices Measure (Gorman-Smith, Tolan, Zelli, & Huesmann, 1996; Tolan, Gorman-Smith, & Henry, 2000). The *Parenting Practices Measure (PPS)* was derived from the parental supervision and discipline interview used in the Oregon Youth Study and Pittsburgh Youth Study (Thornberry, Huizinga, & Loeber, 1995). The *parenting practices measure* measures three major aspects of parenting practices: (1) *Positive Parenting*, (2) *Extent of*

Monitoring and Involvement, and (3) *Discipline Effectiveness.   Positive Parenting* refers to the use of positive rewards and encouragement of appropriate behavior. *Extent of Monitoring and Involvement* pertains to caregiver involvement in daily activities and routines, as well as knowledge of the child's whereabouts. *Discipline Effectiveness* refers to how effective parental discipline is in controlling the child's behavior. *Avoidance of Discipline* measures the parent's disengagement and avoidance of providing consequences for fear of escalating the child's behavior (Tolan et al., 2000).

Items from the *Discipline Effectiveness* and *Avoidance of Discipline* scales tap into how often discipline is effective or avoided using a 3-point scale ranging from 1 (almost never) to 3 (often); items include: "Is the discipline you use effective for your son? Does it work?" Items from the *Positive Parenting Scale* are scored on a 5-point scale ranging from 1 (almost never) to 5 (almost always); items include: "When you have done something that your parents like or approve of, how often does your mother say something nice about it?" Items from the *Supervision and Rules* and *Extent of Involvement* scales are scored on a 4-point scale ranging from 1 (more than 1 month ago) to 4 (yesterday/today); items include: "When was the last time that you talked with your mom about what you had actually done during the day?" *Discipline Effectiveness* is a self-reported measure of how effective the mother's discipline style is in controlling her son's behavior, and *Avoidance of Discipline* refers to the mother's avoidance of providing consequences for her son out of fear of escalation of his behavior (Gorman-Smith, Tolan, Zelli, & Huesmann, 1996). All items in the parenting subscales were scored so that high scores indicated positive parenting. Cronbach's alpha was 0.84 for the *Discipline Avoidance Scale*, 0.69 for the *Discipline Effectiveness Scale*, and 0.87 for the *Monitoring and Involvement Scale* (all assessed using wave 2 data) (Tolan et al., 2000). A confirmatory factor analysis (CFA) was completed for Gorman-Smith, Tolan, Zelli, & Huesmann (1996) with first order scales used as indicators; such scales included *Youth's view of Positive Parenting* and *Extent of Involvement, Mother's View of Positive Parenting* and *Extent of Involvement, Discipline Effectiveness*, and *Discipline Avoidance* (Sheidow, 2000).

The results were consistent with other CYDS papers in identifying latent constructs of Discipline and Monitoring (Gorman-Smith et al., 1996; Sheidow, 2000). In order to develop weightings for factor score computations, the CFA was conducted using wave 2 data. The model was a good fit to the data (X2 (7) = 12.99, p = .07; X2: df = 1.9; RMSEA = .055; GFI = .98; AGFI = .95) (Sheidow, 2000). Next, factor score regression coefficients were obtained using Lisrel in order to generate weightings for the indicator scales; regression coefficients were subsequently used to compute weighted scores for each latent factor. Finally, the unstandardized regression coefficients from the Lisrel analysis were used as the final weightings in creating scores for both Monitoring and Discipline.

Parental Discipline Scores from the *Discipline Effectiveness* and *Avoidance* subscales of the *Parenting Practices Questionnaire* (parent-report) were combined in order to assess the final weighted Discipline construct, based on previous results of a confirmatory factor analysis (see paragraph above for more details). The unstandardized regression coefficients from the Lisrel analysis (described above) were used as the final weightings in the Discipline scores. The final weighted Discipline construct was aggregated across waves 1-4 for the present study was calculated with the following equation: 1.385 + (Mother Avoidance x -0.676) + (Mother Discipline Effectiveness x 0.879) (Sheidow, 2000).

Parental Monitoring Parental monitoring was estimated from aggregating data across waves 1-4 using the final weighted Monitoring construct. The Monitoring construct was calculated based on previous results of a confirmatory factor analysis (see pages 49-50 for details). The final weighted Monitoring construct was calculated with the following equation: 0.040 + (Youth Extent of Involvement x 0.009) + (Youth Positive Parenting x 0.072) + (Caregiver Extent of Involvement x 1.090) + (Caregiver Positive Parenting x 0.385) + (Caregiver Avoidance x 0.262) (Sheidow, 2000).

Mother's Antisocial Behavior Using previously calculated scores from the *CYDS Self-Report Delinquency Measure* (Elliot et al., 1987; Tolan et al., 2002), mothers were assigned a "delinquency" score representing the sum of the frequency of each act multiplied by its weight based on legal seriousness (Tolan et al., 2002). The *Self-Report Delinquency Measure* is described in further detail on pages 45-47. Participants are asked about their engagement in delinquent behavior during the last year, therefore the construct represents present delinquent behavior. Scores ranged from 0 to 4 with higher scores representing a high frequency of violent behavior as well as a high level of seriousness of delinquent acts. In the present study, *mother's antisocial behavior* was estimated from aggregating data across waves 1-4.

<u>Neighborhood Measures and Constructs</u>
Community and Neighborhood Measure (Tolan, Gorman-Smith, & Henry, 2001a). The *Community and Neighborhood Measure* is based on Elliot and colleagues' *Neighborhood Study Measure* (Elliot, Wilson, Huizinga, Sampson, Elliot, & Rankin, 1996). The CYDS measure focuses on six constructs: *Sense of Belonging, Social Support, Perceived Community Problems, Community Involvement, Community Resources Available,* and *Fear of Crime*. Both parents and youth were administered all scales. The measures evaluated individuals' reported experience in the community, neighborhood social qualities that were the context for individual variations in reported experience, and the political economy of the neighborhood thought to contribute to differences in reported neighborhood quality (Tolan et al., 2001a).

The Sense of Belonging scale measures the degree to which the parent and youth feel that they belong to their community. Items include: "I like to think of myself as similar to the people who live in this neighborhood", "I feel like I belong to the neighborhood", "I feel loyal to the neighborhood". *The Social Support scale* measures the degree to which the respondent knows others in the neighborhood and can rely on them for social support. Items include: "If I needed advice about something I could go to someone in my neighborhood", "I would feel comfortable asking to borrow some food or a tool from people on my block", "I visit with neighbors in their homes". Items for the scales above are scored on 5-point Likert scales with responses ranging from Strongly Agree to Strongly Disagree, so that higher numbers indicate greater agreement with items. Cronbach's alpha was 0.76

for mother's report and 0.52 for son's report of *Sense of Belonging*. Cronbach's alpha was 0.80 for mother's report and 0.61 for son's report of *Social Support* (Tolan et al., 2001a).

The Extent of Neighborhood Problems scale measures the degree to which parents and youth perceive crime as a problem in their neighborhood. In assessing *Extent of Neighborhood Problems*, participants were asked whether graffiti, drugs, noise, abandoned buildings, vandalism, burglary, homelessness, gangs, and violent crime were problems in their neighborhood. They were subsequently asked about the extent of the problem using a 5-point Likert scale ranging from 1 to 5 (indicating "a little problem" or "a serious problem", respectively), so that higher numbers indicate that particular crimes are more of a problem in their community. Cronbach's alpha was 0.84 for the mother's report and 0.78 for the son's report of *Perceived Community Problems* (Tolan et al., 2001a).

The Community Involvement scale measures whether or not parent and youth participate in local community organizations. Items include: "I would be willing to work together with others on something to improve my neighborhood", "I am involved in neighborhood or block organizations that deal with neighborhood issues or problems"; the scale is parent-report only. *The Community Resources Available scale* measures whether or not services are available in the community, including medical services, transportation, and entertainment. Items for the scales above are scored as True or False, so that respondents indicate whether or not they are involved in the community and whether or not there are resources available. Cronbach's alpha was 0.62 for the mother's report and 0.49

for the son's report of *Community Involvement*. Cronbach's alpha was 0.74 for mother's report and 0.58 for son's report of *Resources Available* (Tolan et al., 2001a).

Neighborhood Social Processes Neighborhood social processes was assessed with data from mother's and son's reports referring to two previously identified constructs: *Neighborliness* and *Extent of Neighborhood Problems* (Gorman-Smith et al., 2000; Tolan et al., 2003). *Neighborliness* refers to the extent to which respondents see themselves as involved with and able to depend on other community members. Three scales have been used as indicators of *Neighborliness* (a) *Sense of Belonging*; (b) *Social Support*; and (c) *Community Involvement* (parent-report only). Cronbach's alpha for mother's reports for the three scales was 0.76 (*Sense of Belonging*), 0.80 (*Social Support*), and 0.62 (*Community Involvement*). Cronbach's alpha for son's reports for the first two scales was 0.52 (*Sense of Belonging*) and 0.61 (*Social Support*) (Tolan et al., 2003). *Neighborhood Problems* have been assessed using the *Extent of Neighborhood Problems* scale described above, which measures the degree to which crimes are perceived as problematic in the respondent's neighborhood. *Neighborhood Social Processes* was estimated from aggregating data from waves 1-4.

Neighborhood Resources The *Community Resources Available Scale* from the *CYDS Community and Neighborhood Measure* (Tolan, Gorman-Smith, & Henry, 2001a) was used to assess *neighborhood resources* (Tolan & Gorman-Smith, 1993). Specifically, subscales measuring resource availability and use were used; such items were selected to reflect the political economy of the neighborhood (Tolan & Gorman-Smith, 1993). Items from the *Resources Available* subscale included: "There is a grocery store in or near my neighborhood", "There is a clinic or other medical services near my neighborhood". Items from the *Use of Community Resources* subscale included: "I regularly do my shopping in my neighborhood", "When I need medical services, I use those in my neighborhood" (Tolan & Gorman-Smith, 1993). Items were answered "yes" or "no" by respondents, and were scored as 1 or 0 respectively. Cronbach's alpha was 0.74 for the mother's report and 0.58 for the son's report of the *Resources Available Scale* (assessed using wave 2 data) (Tolan et al., 2001a). *Neighborhood resources* was assessed by aggregating data from waves 1-4.

Exposure to Violence Measure (Tolan & Gorman-Smith, 1992). *The Exposure to Violence Interview* is a subscale within the *Stress and Coping Measure* (Tolan & Gorman-Smith, 1992), and consists of nine items related to witnessing violence and victimization. Participants were asked if they had ever witnessed the events in the questionnaire during the last year. Items include: "Has a family member been robbed or attacked (beaten up, raped, or otherwise hurt intentionally) by someone?" If the participant indicated that such an event had taken place during the last year, they were asked where the event took place, the specifics of the incident, and his relationship to the victim and perpetrator. Report of events taking place during their lifetime, as well as the frequency during the last year, were obtained from participants (Tolan & Gorman-Smith, 1992).

Exposure to Neighborhood Violence Exposure to violence was assessed as a total frequency count for six events from *the Exposure to Violence Interview*, a subscale of the *CYDS Stress and Coping Measure* (Brady, Gorman-Smith, Henry, & Tolan, 2008; Tolan & Gorman-Smith, 1991). The six events assessed were as follows: (1) Anyone in your family was robbed or attached (beaten up, raped, or hurt by someone); (2) Someone else you know, other than a member of your family, gotten beaten, attached or really hurt by others; (2) You saw anyone beaten up; (4) You saw anyone shot or killed; (5) You were the victim of any violent crime involving force or threat of force; (6) You witnessed any violent crime (not counting what you have already told me about). Consistent with previous CYDS studies, three items were omitted because answers to such questions could reflect an experience other than community violence exposure (Brady et al., 2008). Omitted items were: (1) A close friend of yours was killed; (2) You were the victim of a non-violent crime; (3) You were the victim of a sexual assault. Reported frequencies for each event were recoded using the scale: 0: none, 1: once, and 2: more than once, and mean scores were computed across six events, resulting in an overall score for each participant ranging from 0-2 (Brady et al., 2008). *Exposure to neighborhood violence* was assessed by aggregating data from waves 2-4, as data on exposure to street violence was not collected in wave 1.

Control Variables
There is evidence that both family socioeconomic status and ethnic group are related to delinquency and antisocial behavior (Lipsey & Derzon, 1999). Sampson and Laub (1993) demonstrated that family socioeconomic status and maternal employment were associated with juvenile delinquency, both directly and through the impact of family

social control mechanisms. In addition, socioeconomic disadvantage and poverty have been shown to adversely impact parenting practices, contended to make it difficult to sustain adaptive patterns of parenting (Broidy et al., 2003). Furthermore, there is evidence that the impact of family processes on antisocial behavior differs by ethnic group. Henry, Tolan, and Gorman-Smith (2001) found that the path from family type to gang membership was significant for African American participants, but not for Hispanic participants. In addition, although all CYDS participants reside in distressed urban neighborhoods, African American participants are more likely than Hispanics to live in public housing projects (Henry et al., 2001), which could differentially influence exposure to neighborhood stressors between racial groups. Previous evidence for the influence of socioeconomic status and ethnic group on delinquency support the purpose of controlling for such factors in the present study.

Data on ethnic group were obtained from both mother and son reports on ethnic group. Socioeconomic status was assessed using mother's education level at baseline, and was controlled for in all reported analyses. Ethnic group was measured as a dichotomous variable, such that African American participants received a score of 0 and Hispanic American participants received a score of 1. The Hispanic participants were grouped together based on the reason that nearly all were of Mexican American ethnic group (Henry et al., 2001).

OVERVIEW OF ANALYTIC STRATEGY

The primary goal of the present study was to examine how various individual, family, and neighborhood factors assessed during adolescence were associated with desistance from crime in young adulthood. In addition, the present study examined predictors of desistance among low-income African-American and Hispanic males from inner-city communities. Preliminary analyses were conducted to evaluate skewness of the study variables; skewed variables were subsequently transformed to normalize the variables. In addition, bivariate correlations among study variables were examined in order to determine whether there were issues of multicollinearity.

Following the preliminary analyses, study hypotheses were tested using a series of stepwise binary logistic regression models to examine predictors of desistance from antisocial behavior in young adulthood. Binary logistic regression is an appropriate technique when modeling associations between explanatory variables and binary dependent outcomes. As desistance was measured as a dichotomous variable, binary logistic regression was ultimately used. The initial analyses assessed the unique effects of aggression, impulsivity, parental discipline, parental monitoring, mother's antisocial behavior, neighborhood social processes, neighborhood resources, and exposure to violence on odds of desisting from crime.

Ethnic group and mother's education were entered as control variables at Step 1 and were retained for all subsequent analyses. Key individual characteristics were entered at Step 2 to test whether individual characteristics aggregated over waves 1-4 significantly influence odds of desistance. Individual characteristics were hypothesized to be negatively associated with desistance, and aggression was associated to be a stronger risk factor relative to impulsivity for persistent antisocial behavior. Key family variables were entered at Step 3 to test whether such family characteristics aggregated over waves 1-4 aided in explaining odds of desisting (over and above control variables and individual characteristics). Family protective factors (e.g., parental discipline and monitoring) were hypothesized to be positively associated with desistance. Conversely, mother's antisocial behavior was hypothesized to be negatively associated with desistance. The family variables were entered before the neighborhood constructs in an effort to account for proximal effects on antisocial behavior before attributing effects to neighborhood-based factors (Duncan, et al., 1997).

Key neighborhood structural characteristics were entered at Step 4, to test whether neighborhood characteristics aggregated over waves 1-4 aided in explaining odds of desisting in crime (above and beyond covariates, individual characteristics, and family characteristics). Neighborhood risk factors (e.g., exposure to violence) were hypothesized to be negatively associated with desistance, while neighborhood protective factors (e.g., resources and social cohesion) were hypothesized to be positively associated with desistance. Exposure to violence was aggregated over waves 2-4, as the street violence scale was administered first to youth participants in wave 2.

Additionally, interactions between individual, family, and neighborhood processes were entered at Step 5 to test hypotheses about the impact of impulsivity, aggression, and discipline in relation to the moderating effect of other variables. A moderator is defined as a variable that qualifies the association between a predictor and an outcome variable (Aiken & West, 1991); therefore, the effect of the predictor on the outcome changes depending on the impact of the moderator variable. Identifying significant moderators allows researchers to demonstrate processes by which certain factors amplify or reduce the influence of other key variables. Several predictions about moderation were tested in the present study. First, aggression was hypothesized to exacerbate the effect of impulsivity on desistance. Specifically, impulsivity was predicted to be a stronger risk factor for persistence in highly aggressive youths. In addition, discipline was hypothesized to buffer the association between aggression and desistance, and was predicted to be a stronger protective factor for highly aggressive youths. Lastly, exposure to violence was hypothesized to exacerbate the effect of aggression on desistance, as well as to moderate the association between parental discipline and desistance. It is likely that the broader neighborhood ecology within which families reside moderates the effect of parenting on child outcomes (Leventhal & Brooks-Gunn, 2000; McLoyd, 1998); thus, family effects may not be independent of the neighborhood context. Although some studies have shown that parenting has a stronger impact on adolescent outcomes in high-risk neighborhoods (Cleveland et al., 2005), there is also evidence that exposure to neighborhood risk may weaken the impact of positive parenting (Sheidow et al., 2001). Furthermore, in high-crime neighborhoods, the positive impact of parenting may be overpowered by deleterious neighborhoods effects. Therefore, the positive association between discipline and desistance was hypothesized to be stronger for youth exposed to low levels of neighborhood violence. As shown in Table 6, two-way interactions were tested between impulsivity and aggression, aggression and parental discipline, aggression and exposure to neighborhood violence, and between parental discipline and exposure to violence.

Furthermore, non-significant predictors were trimmed from the final model in order to achieve parsimony. As shown in Table 7, aggression, discipline, mother's antisocial behavior, exposure to violence, and the interaction between aggression and discipline were tested in the final model. Although mother's antisocial behavior was not statistically significant, the p-value was low enough that it was retained and tested with the significant covariates. Subsequently, the interaction between aggression and parental discipline was probed by centering the predictor variables and analyzing the association between aggression and desistance at high, medium, and low levels of parental discipline. As shown in Figure 1, the significant interaction was also graphed in order to facilitate interpretation of the association between variables tested.

Lastly, post-hoc mediation analyses were conducted to further examine whether there were third variables present that explained significant main effects (see Figures 2-4). A mediator is defined as an intervening variable that accounts for the association between a predictor and an outcome variable (Baron & Kenny, 1986); therefore, the predictor is said to influence the outcome indirectly via a mediating variable that accounts for part or all of the association. Identifying significant mediators allows researchers to understand the mechanisms that directly and indirectly impact developmental outcomes. Baron and Kenny (1986) suggested four requisite conditions for defining a significant mediation. The first condition is that the independent variable must be significantly associated with the mediator variable. Next, the predictor variable must be significantly associated with the outcome variable. In addition, the mediator must be significantly associated with the outcome variable. Finally, the effect of the predictor variable on the outcome variable must be less once the mediator is in the model. If there is full mediation, then the association between the predictor and the outcome will become non-significant once the mediator is added into the model; furthermore, if there is partial mediation, the association between the predictor and the outcome variable will remain significant, but will decrease in strength. Specifically, mother's antisocial behavior was tested as a mediator of direct effects from aggression and parental discipline. In addition, discipline was tested as a mediator of the direct association between exposure to neighborhood violence and desistance. Although several mediation models were tested, only those that were statistically significant or that approached significance are discussed in detail.

Chapter Four
Findings for Risk and Protective Factors Influencing Desistance

<u>Means and Standard Deviations</u>
The means and standard deviations were calculated for all covariates, individual, family, and neighborhood variables are presented in Table 3. Descriptive statistics were reflective of the high-risk nature of the study sample; of the key variables, aggression, impulsivity, mother's antisocial behavior and exposure to violence had exceptionally high skewness statistics. Skewness statistics approaching zero indicate normality of the distribution. With samples smaller than 200, it is particularly important to evaluate skewness of the distribution because it can make a substantive difference in the analysis. The skewness and kurtosis values were evaluated for the major study variables, and the distribution was also inspected using a histogram. Aggression, impulsivity, mother's antisocial behavior, and exposure to violence all had a moderate right skew; therefore, a square root transformation was performed which resulted in a considerable reduction in their skewness in order to normalize the variables. As shown in

Table 3, the transformed variables approached a normal distribution following the procedure, and were used in place of the original variables in all subsequent analyses.

As shown in Tables 1 and 2, descriptive statistics for demographic variables and key study variables are presented for desisters and persisters in the sample. Desisters are characterized by having mothers with higher educational attainment (μ = 4.03, ∂ = 1.45), and also have lower mean levels of aggression (μ = 2.29, ∂ = .47) and impulsivity (μ = 2.00, ∂ = .49), compared with persisters. Furthermore, desisters are exposed to higher levels of parental monitoring (μ = -.03, ∂ = .31), higher levels of parental discipline (μ = .08, ∂ = .24), and lower levels of mother's antisocial behavior (μ = .68, ∂ = .32). Finally, desisters report living in neighborhoods with stronger social cohesion (μ = 3.09, ∂ = .37), more resources (μ = 1.40, ∂ = .49), and less exposure to violence (μ = .51, ∂ = .26).

Conversely, persisters are characterized with having mothers with lower educational attainment (μ = 3.88, ∂ = 1.32), and also have higher mean levels of aggression (μ = 2.51, ∂ = .48) and impulsivity (μ = 2.08, ∂ = .42), compared with their desister counterparts. Moreover, persisters are exposed to lower levels of parental monitoring (μ = -.07, ∂ = .33), lower levels of parental discipline (μ = .03, ∂ = .29), and higher levels of mother's antisocial behavior (μ = .80, ∂ = .39). In addition, persisters report living in neighborhoods with weaker social cohesion (μ = 3.0, ∂ = .40), less neighborhood resources (μ = 1.37, ∂ = .43), and more exposure to violence (μ = .55, ∂ = .23).

Table 3. Descriptive Statistics for Key Study Variables

Variable	N	Mean (SD) Pre-T	Mean (SD) Post-T	Skewness Pre-T	Range Pre-T	Range Post-T	Skewness Post-T
Ethnic Group	190	1.49 (.895)	----	3.24 (.18)	1.00 – 8.00	----	----
Mother's Education	168	3.97 (1.38)	----	.277 (.19)	1.00 – 7.00	----	----
Aggression	196	6.28 (2.57)	2.46 (.50)	.87 (.17)	2.07 - 15.87	1.44 – 3.98	.33 (.17)
Impulsivity	196	4.54 (2.12)	2.08 (.48)	1.18 (.17)	1.00 – 12.50	1.00 – 3.54	.44 (.17)
Parental Discipline	196	.08 (.27)	----	-.014 (.17)	-.79 - .82	----	----
Parental Monitoring	196	-.07 (.32)	----	-.75 (.17)	-1.15 - .52	----	----
Mother's AB	196	.75 (.61)	.79 (.36)	1.14 (.17)	0 – 3.00	0 – 1.73	.15 (.17)
Social Processes	196	3.04 (.39)	----	.04 (.17)	2.11 – 4.04	----	----
Resources	196	1.38 (.46)	----	-.06 (.17)	0.31 - 2.34	----	----
Exposure to Viol	196	0.38 (.26)	0.56 (.24)	.86 (.17)	0 – 1.33	0 – 1.15	-.42 (.17)
Desistance	136	0.55 (.50)	----	-.21 (.21)	0 - 1	----	----
Valid N	118						

Note. In order to reduce skewness, Aggression, Impulsivity, Mother's AB and Exposure to Violence variables were transformed using a square root transformation. The remaining variables listed were not transformed. T = Transformation; Mother's AB = Mother's Antisocial Behavior; Social Processes = Neighborhood Social Processes;_ Resources = Neighborhood Resources; Exposure to Viol = Exposure to Violence.

Ethnicity seemed evenly distributed between desisters and persister categories. The descriptive statistics presented in Tables 1 and 2 confirm the direction of the study hypotheses, underscoring the rationale behind testing risk factors such as aggression, impulsivity, mother's antisocial behavior, and exposure to violence, as they are shown to be more prevalent among males who persist in crime. Finally, the descriptive statistics additionally confirm the motivation for testing promotive factors such as parental monitoring, discipline, neighborhood social processes and neighborhood resources, as such factors are more prevalent among males who desist in young adulthood.

Intercorrelations

After calculating descriptive statistics for the variables of interest, the bivariate correlations were examined among the study variables to determine whether there were issues of multicollinearity to be addressed. The zero-order correlations among the study variables are presented in Table 4. Correlation analyses revealed that about half of the associations between study variables were non-significant; as shown in Table 4, the associations that were statistically significant were typically small, suggesting few issues of overlap between analytic constructs and measures used. The largest correlation emerged between aggression and impulsivity,_ and the next largest correlations emerged between parental discipline and desistance and between aggression and mother's antisocial behavior. The correlation between discipline and monitoring was the next largest, followed by the correlation between aggression and desistance (see Table 4 for details). Collinearity statistics were also examined, and all tolerance statistics were over

0.40, indicating no issues with multicollinearity in the regression equations. Tolerance values below 0.10 indicate that the variable has high correlations with other variables in the model, and should therefore be reconsidered (Cohen, Cohen, West, & Aiken, 2003).

Correlations were consistent with past research indicating that measures of childhood impulsivity are predictive of antisocial behaviors across childhood and into adulthood (Caspi, 2000; Farrington & Welsh, 2007). Furthermore, correlations were consistent with literature indicating that childhood aggression is a strong indicator of antisocial propensity and risk for desistance (Gottfredson & Hirschi, 1990; Moffitt et al., 2002). Correlations were also consistent with research indicating that problematic parenting, mother's antisocial behavior, and neighborhood violence are correlated with aggression as well as with later delinquency and violence (Sampson & Laub, 1997; Farrington et al., 1996). Consistent with previous research (Tolan et al., 2003) neighborhood resources and social processes were also positively correlated to one another; in addition, social processes was negatively correlated to exposure to violence.

Model Summaries

Table 5 reports the model fit statistics for binary logistic analyses conducted. The full model containing all predictors and interactions was statistically significant, $\chi2$ $(_{df}\ 14,\ 118) = 35.91$, $(p > .001)$ In addition, the final trimmed model was also statistically significant, $\chi2$ $(_{df}\ 7,\ 118) = 33.73$, $(p < .001)$, indicating that both models were able to adequately identify respondents who desisted. The analyses revealed a consistent increase in the variance explained at each step of the logistic regression analyses,

Table 4. Intercorrelations Among Key Study Variables

		1	2	3	4	5	6	7	8	9	10
1	Ethnic group	-									
2	Mother Ed	-.07	-								
3	Aggression	.08	-.21**	-							
4	Impulsivity	.17*	-.16*	.66**	-						
5	Mother AB	-.19**	.11	.33**	.14*	-					
6	Discipline	-.05	.03	-.20**	-.07	-.13	-				
7	Monitoring	-.11	.11	-.19**	-.06	-.14	.31**	-			
8	ExpToViol	-.02	.13	.29**	.06	.18*	-.12	-.03	-		
9	Resources	.17*	..17*	-.03	-.02	-.12	.01	.02	.02	-	
10	Social Proc	.21**	.15	-.16*	-.04	-.20**	-.03	.00	-.17**	.29**	-
11	Desistance	.02	.02	-.30**	-.16	-.41*	.33**	.154	-.28**	.05	.11

Note. Mother Ed = Mother's Education; Mother AB = Mother's antisocial behavior; Discipline = Parental Discipline; Monitoring = Parental Monitoring; ExpToViol = Exposure to Violence; Resources = Neighborhood Resources; Social Proc = Neighborhood Social Processes.

* = *p*< .05; ** = *p*< .01; *** = *p* < .001

indicated by the Cox and Snell (1989) R^2 estimate, Nagelkerke (1991) R^2 estimate, and the R^2 change statistics. In the full logistic regression model, predictors and interaction terms explained between 26 percent (Cox and Snell R^2) and 35 percent (Nagelkerke R^2) of the variability in desistance. In the trimmed logistic regression model, predictors explained between 25percent (Cox and Snell R^2) and 33 percent (Nagelkerke R^2) of the variability in desistance.

The Positive Predictive Value (PPV) is also displayed in Table 5, indicating the percentage of cases that the model classifies correctly as possessing the hypothesized characteristic(s). The PPV of both the full and trimmed models was the highest at Step 5, with all individual, family, and neighborhood main effects and interactions being tested. The overall positive predictive value was 79.4 percent for the full regression model, and 81.5 percent for the trimmed regression model, indicating some change in the precision of the trimmed model over the full model.

FULL ANALYTIC MODELS

<u>Main Effects</u>
Results from a one way analysis of variance (ANOVA) indicated that both ethnic group and mother's education had significant subgroup differences in predicting the outcome variable. However, participant age was neither significantly associated with desistance, nor were there significant subgroup differences based on participant age with regards to desistance. Therefore, ethnic group and mother's education were retained and entered at Step 1 as control variables for all subsequent regression analysis.

Table 5. Model Fit Statistics for Full and Trimmed Models

Model/ Step	Overall Model Evaluation			Goodness of Fit: Hosmer &Omnibus Tests of Model Coefficients		
	Cox & Snell R^2	Nagelkerke R^2 (R^2 Change)	Positive Predictive Value (PPV)	χ^2	df	p-value
Full Model						
Step 1: Covariates	.00	.00 (.00)	55.9%	.03	2	.98
Step 2: Individual Factors	.12	.16 (.16)	66.2%	14.53	4	.01 **
Step 3: Family Factors	.20	.27 (.11)	73.6%	26.63	7	.00 ***
Step 4: Neighborhood Fx	.23	.31 (.04)	75.0%	30.74	10	.00 ***
Step 5: Interactions	.26	.35 (.04)	79.4%	35.91	14	.00 ***
Final Model						
Step 1: Covariates	.00	.00 (.00)	55.9%	.03	2	.98
Step 2: Individual Factors	.12	.15 (.15)	65.4 %	14.39	3	.00**
Step 3: Family Factors	.20	.27 (.12)	70.3%	26.37	5	.00***
Step 4: Neighborhood Fx	.22	.30 (.03)	71.6%	29.82	6	.00 ***
Step 5: Interactions	.25	.33 (.03)	81.5%	33.73	7	.00 ***

Note. Neighborhood Fx = Neighborhood Factors

* = $p < .05$; ** = $p < .01$; *** = $p < .001$

 Ethnic group and mother's education did not significantly influence likelihood of desistance when main effects were tested.

Individual Characteristics

After entering the control variables, aggression and impulsivity were entered to test whether such individual characteristics were significantly associated with desistance. As shown in Table 6, aggression measured across adolescence was a strong negative predictor of desistance in young adulthood (β = -1.694, $p <$ .01). As indicated by the odds ratio (OR = 0.18), for each unit increase in the aggression score, the odds of desistance decreased from 1.0 to 0.18. As shown in Table 4 the aggression construct had narrow variation post-transformation (μ = 2.456, ∂ = 0.502), suggesting that the odds ratio reported corresponds to an approximate 2 standard deviation increase in aggression. Contrary to the research hypotheses, impulsivity was not significantly associated with desistance; therefore, impulsivity was omitted from the final model in an effort to achieve parsimony.

Family Processes

Parental discipline, parental monitoring, and mother's antisocial behavior were entered next to test whether such family variables were significantly associated with desistance from crime. As shown in Table 6, parental discipline measured across adolescence was a strong positive predictor of desistance in young adulthood (β = 2.29, $p <$ .05. As indicated by the odds ratio (OR = 9.89), for each unit increase in the parental discipline, the odds of

                                                          Desistance

desistance increased from 1.0 to 9.89. As shown in Table 6, the parental discipline construct had particularly narrow variation (μ = 0.078, ∂ = 0.273), suggesting that the odds ratio reported corresponds to an approximate 32.9 standard deviation increase in parental discipline, which should be noted as particularly large. Contrary to the research hypotheses, parental monitoring was not significantly associated with desistance; therefore, parental monitoring was omitted from the final model. As shown in Table 6, mother's antisocial behavior measured across adolescence was not a statistically significant negative predictor of desistance (ß = -1.19, *p* = .13); however, because the p-value approached significance, mother's antisocial behavior was kept in the final model.

Neighborhood Structural Characteristics
Neighborhood social processes,_ neighborhood resources, and exposure to violence were entered next to test whether such neighborhood characteristics were significantly associated with desistance. Contrary to the research hypotheses, neighborhood social processes and neighborhood resources were not significantly associated with desistance; therefore neighborhood social processes and neighborhood resources were omitted from the final model. As shown in Table 6, exposure to violence measured across adolescence approached significance as a negative predictor of desistance in young adulthood (ß = -1.84, *p* = .06). As indicated by the odds ratio (OR = 0.16), for each unit increase in the exposure to violence, the odds of desistance decreased from 1.0 to 0.16. As shown in Table 3, the exposure to violence construct had narrow variation post-transformation (μ = 0.376, ∂ = 0.261), suggesting that

the odds ratio reported corresponds to an approximate 3.2 standard deviation increase in exposure to violence.

The initial analyses assessed the unique effects of aggression, impulsivity, parental discipline, parental monitoring, mother's antisocial behavior, neighborhood social processes, neighborhood resources, and exposure to violence on odds of desisting from crime. Thus, there were a total of eight main effects tested in the full model (discounting covariates). When individual, family, and neighborhood effects were tested together in Step 4, parental discipline was the strongest predictor of desistance, recording an odds ratio of 11.992 ($ß$ = 2.48, p < .05). This indicated that for one unit increase in parental discipline, the odds of desistance increased from 1.0 to 11.992, controlling for other factors in the model. Mother's antisocial behavior was consistently not statistical significant in the final step of the model, ($ß$ = -1.120, p > .05). Interestingly, aggression was no longer a significant predictor after family and neighborhood factors were accounted for.

<u>Interactions</u>
Four one-way interactions were tested between individual, family, and neighborhood factors, as can be seen in Table 6. Aggression was tested as a moderator of the association between impulsivity and desistance. Participants with high levels of impulsivity were hypothesized to have a low chance of desisting from crime only when coupled with high levels of aggression; in other words, aggression was predicted to exacerbate risk from impulsivity on persistence. Contrary to the initial hypotheses, there was no significant interaction between impulsivity and aggression

in predicting probability of desistance. Next, parental discipline was tested as a moderator of the association between aggression and desistance. Positive parenting was hypothesized to buffer risk from aggression, and highly aggressive youth were hypothesized to have a lower chance of desisting when exposed to poor parenting. As predicted, the interaction between aggression and parental discipline was significant in predicting desistance.

Exposure to violence was then tested as a moderator of the association between aggression and desistance. Exposure to violence was hypothesized to exacerbate risk from aggression. Contrary to the hypotheses, there was no significant interaction between aggression and exposure to violence in predicting desistance. Finally, exposure to violence was tested as a moderator of the association between parental discipline and desistance. Neighborhood risk level was hypothesized to moderate the association between parental discipline and desistance from crime. Specifically, exposure to violence was hypothesized to exacerbate risk from poor parental discipline. Contrary to the hypotheses, exposure to violence did not significantly moderate the association between parental discipline and desistance.

FINAL ANALYTIC MODELS

Main Effects
In the final model, non-significant predictors were trimmed in order to achieve parsimony; however, covariates were retained based on their subgroup differences related to the outcome. In the final model presented in Table 7, main effects were tested for aggression, parental discipline,

Table 6. Binary Logistic Regression Results for Full Analytic Model

Regression Step	Variable	B (SE)	B (SE) Final Step	OR	Probability	Wald Test	95% CI For Exp (B)	
							Lower	Upper
Step 1: Covariates								
	Ethnic Group	-.02 (.19)	-.05(.22)	.098	49%	.02	.68	1.4
	Mother's Ed	.02 (.13)	-.05 (.16)	1.02	51%	.02	.78	1.32
Step 2 : Indiv Fx								
	Aggression	-1.69 (.58)**	-.72 (.69)	.18	16%	8.49	.06	.57
	Impulsivity	.23 (.55)	-.29 (.61)	1.26	6%	.18	.43	3.70
Step 3: Family Fx								
	Discipline	2.29 (.98)*	2.48 (1.00)*	9.89	91%	5.46	1.45	67.62
	Monitoring	.34 (.69)	.23 (.71)	1.40	17%	.24	.36	5.46
	Mother AB	-1.19 (.73)	-1.12(.76)	.30	23%	2.66	.07	1.27

Table 6. Binary Logistic Regression Results for Full Analytic Model (Continued)

Regression Step	Variable	B (SE)	B (SE) Final Step	OR	Probability	Wald Test	95% CI For Exp (B) Lower	Upper
Step 4: Nbrhd Fx								
	SocialProc	-.12 (.65)	-.12 (.65)	.89	47%	.04	.25	3.15
	Resources	.37 (.53)	.37 (.53)	1.45	59%	.49	.51	4.10
	ExpToViol	-1.84 (1.04), p = .06	-1.84 (1.04), p = .06	.16	14%	3.14	.02	1.22
Step 5: Interact's								
	Imp x Agg	.01 (.82)	\	.1.01	50%	.00	.20	5.03
	Agg x Disc	.72 (.42)*	\	.49	33%	3.00	.22	1.10
	Agg x ETV	1.89 (2.3)	\	6.36	86%	.63	.07	624.86
	Disc x ETV	4.33 (5.5)		75.71	99%	.63	.00	3437641.87

Note. Indiv Fx = Individual Factors, Family Fx = Family Factors, Nbrhd Fx = Neighborhood Factors, Interact's = Interactions; EthnicGrp = Ethnic Group, Mother Ed = Mother's Education; Discipline = Parental Discipline, Monitoring = Parental Monitoring, Mother AB = Mother's antisocial behavior; ExpToViol = Exposure to Violence, Resources = Neighborhood Resources, SocialProc = Neighborhood Social Processes; Imp x Agg = Impulsivity x Aggression interaction term, Agg x Disc = Aggression x Discipline interaction term, Agg x ETV = Aggression x Exposure to Violence interaction term, Disc x ETV = Discipline x Exposure to Violence interaction term.

* = $p< .05$; ** = $p< .01$; *** = $p < .001$

Table 7. Binary Logistic Regression Results for Final Analytic Model

Regression Step	Variable	B (SE)	B (SE) Final Step	OR	Probability	Wald Test	95% CI For Exp (B) Lower	Upper
Step 1: Covariates								
	Ethnic Group	-.02 (.19)	-.07 (.22)	.098	49%	.02	.68	1.40
	Mother's Ed	.02 (.13)	-.05 (.17)	1.02	51%	.02	.78	1.32
Step 2 : Indiv Fx								
	Aggression	-1.54 (.44)***	-.62 (.52)	.22	18%	12.37	.09	.51
Step 3: Family Fx								
	Discipline	2.44 (.90)**	2.44 (.90)**	11.31	92%	7.21	1.93	66.45
	Mother AB	-1.18 (.73)	-1.8 (1.0)	.12	11%	2.62	.07	1.28

Table 7. Binary Logistic Regression Results for Final Analytic Model (Continued)

Regression Step	Variable	B (SE)	B (SE) Final Step	OR	Probability	Wald Test	95% CI For Exp (B)	
							Lower	Upper
Step 4: Nbrhd Fx								
	ExpToViol	-1.80 (1.0)*	-1.80 (1.0)*	.17	15%	3.26	.023	1.17
Step 5: Interact's								
	Agg x Disc	-.75 (.39)*	--	.47	32%	3.73	.22	1.01

Note. Individual Fx = Individual Factors, Family Fx = Family Factors, Neighbrhd Fx = Neighborhood Factors; Mother Ed = Mother's Education; Discipline = Parental Discipline, Mother AB = Mother's antisocial behavior; ExpToViol = Exposure to Violence, Agg x Disc = Aggression x Discipline interaction term, Agg x ETV = Aggression x Exposure to Violence interaction term. * = $p< .05$; ** = $p< .01$; *** = $p < .001$

mother's antisocial behavior and exposure to violence in explaining odds of desistance from crime. Thus, there were a total of four main effects examined in the final model (discounting covariates). As hypothesized, aggression measured across adolescence was a strong negative predictor of desistance in young adulthood (ß = -1.54, *p*< .001). As indicated by the odds ratio (OR = 0.22), for each unit increase in the aggression score, the odds of desistance decreased from 1.0 to 0.22. Also as predicted, parental discipline measured across adolescence was a strong positive predictor of desistance in young adulthood (ß = 2.44, *p* < .01). As indicated by the odds ratio (OR = 11.31), for each unit increase in the parental discipline score, the odds of desistance increased from 1.0 to 11.31. As discussed previously, and shown in Table 2, the discipline construct had particularly narrow variation, which explains the large odds ratio recorded. In addition, mother's antisocial behavior still only approached significance as a negative predictor of desistance (ß = -1.18, *p* = .12). As indicated by the odds ratio (OR = 0.12), for each unit increase in the mother's antisocial behavior score, the odds of desistance approached significance in decreasing from 1.0 to 0.12. Furthermore, exposure to neighborhood violence measured across adolescence was a significant negative predictor of desistance in young adulthood in the final model (ß = -1.80, *p* < .05), which was also consistent with the research hypotheses. As indicated by the odds ratio (OR = 0.17), for each unit increase in the exposure to violence score, the odds of desistance decreased from 1 to 0.17. As discussed previously, and shown in Table 3, the violence construct had particularly narrow variation post-transformation, which explains the large odds ratio recorded.

When individual, family, and neighborhood effects were tested together in Step 4 of the final model, parental discipline was the strongest predictor of desistance from crime, recording an odds ratio of 11.63 (ß = 2.44, *p* < .01). This indicated that for each unit increase in parental discipline, odds of desistance increased from 1.0 to 11.63, controlling for other factors in the model. Mother's antisocial behavior also remained non-significance in the final step of the model (ß = -1.8, *p* > .05). Consistent with the full analytic model, aggression was no longer a significant predictor after family and neighborhood factors were accounted for.

Interactions
Moderator variables are said to alter the strength of an association between a predictor and outcome (Baron & Kenny, 1986). In addition, moderation can be used to describe the weakening, amplification, or nullification of a direct relation between variables (Baron & Kenny, 1986). In the present study, interactions were entered at the final step, in order to control for the lower order main effects (Cohen, 1987). Because the interaction between aggression and parental discipline was statistically significant in predicting an increase in desistance, this interaction was tested again in the final logistic regression model and subsequently analyzed in further depth. As shown in Table 7, aggression was entered at Step 2, followed by parental discipline and mother's antisocial behavior at Step 3, followed by exposure to violence at Step 4, followed by the interaction term between aggression and parental discipline at Step 5. As predicted, parental discipline significantly moderated the association between aggression and

desistance and was therefore decomposed to better understand the structure of the association. In addition, the R^2 coefficient from Step 4 of the final model was between 22-30%, subsequently increasing to between 25-33% after the interaction was introduced. Therefore, there was an approximate 3% increase in the fit of the model after the interaction between aggression and discipline was included (shown in Table 5).

In order to examine the interaction, the predictor variables were centered by subtracting the mean from each value, thus creating new centered variables. The predictors were centered in order to reduce nonessential multicollinearity among predictors, which can arise when interaction terms and their component predictor variables are tested in the same model (Aiken & West, 1991). In addition, the predictors were centered in order to facilitate interpretation of the main effects and of the interaction results. The only exception to the advantages of centering is if the predictor has a meaningful zero point (Aiken & West, 1991), which was not the case for either the aggression or parental discipline variables.

After centering the predictors and re-calculating the interaction terms, binary logistic regression was conducted to investigate associations with desistance. As shown in Table 7, the coefficient for aggression represents the overall significant negative effect of aggression on desistance. As indicated by the odds ratio (OR = .22), for each unit increase in the aggression score, the odds of desistance decreased from 1.0 to .22. In addition, the coefficient for parental discipline represents the overall significant positive effect of discipline on desistance. As indicated by the odds ratio (OR = 11.31), for each unit increase in the discipline score, the odds of desistance increased from 1.0 to 11.31.As anticipated, the interaction between aggression and parental discipline maintained statistical significance after the centering procedure.

In addition, the interaction was probed by examining the association between aggression and desistance at high levels of parental discipline and at low levels of parental discipline. The results shown in Figure 1 indicate an unanticipated pattern following the interaction probing. At high levels of parental discipline, the association between aggression and desistance was statistically significant; however, at low levels of parental discipline, the association between aggression and desistance was not significant. Moreover, at medium to high levels of parental discipline, aggression is strongly negatively associated with desistance, indicating that for the highly aggressive youth, parental discipline is a risk factor for persistence in crime.

In order to further improve interpretation of the interaction,_ a graphical representation of the interaction is displayed in Figure 1; the graph confirms the interpretation of the association between variables tested. For youth with low levels of aggression, parental discipline was not significantly associated with odds of desisting from crime. However, for youth with high levels of aggression, parental discipline did not promote desistance from crime. On the contrary, youth with high levels of aggression were actually less likely to desist from offending when they experienced medium to high levels of parental discipline. The direction of this finding was counter to the hypothesis that parental discipline would buffer risk for desistance in highly aggressive youth. As shown in Table 12, a cross-tabulation was conducted to examine how many participants were represented in each group. Results demonstrated that there were a total of 88 participants who were classified as having high levels of aggression and being exposed to medium and high levels of parental discipline, thus representing approximately 45% of the total sample. Of the 97 participants classified as having high levels of aggression, 16 were exposed to high levels of parental discipline, representing approximately 8% of the total sample. The role of parental discipline in predicting persistence was significant only for highly aggressive participants exposed to medium and high levels of discipline. Although only 8% of the sample had high levels of aggression and high levels of discipline, close to 45% of the highly aggressive participants were at greater risk for persistence based on their exposure to medium to high levels of discipline. Explanations for this interaction finding are elaborated on in the discussion section.

<u>Mediators</u>
After testing the main effects and interactions, three mediation models were examined, thus presented in Figures 2, 3, and 4. As shown previously in Tables 6 and 7, aggression became a non-significant risk factor after accounting for family and neighborhood factors; therefore, post-hoc mediation models were tested in order to better understand whether there were third variables that could explain risk from aggression on persistent antisocial behavior. In addition, parental discipline was shown to be a consistently strong predictor of later desistance; therefore, mediation models were also tested to explain the effect of discipline on desistance.

Figure 1. Graphical Representation of Interaction between Aggression and Parental Discipline

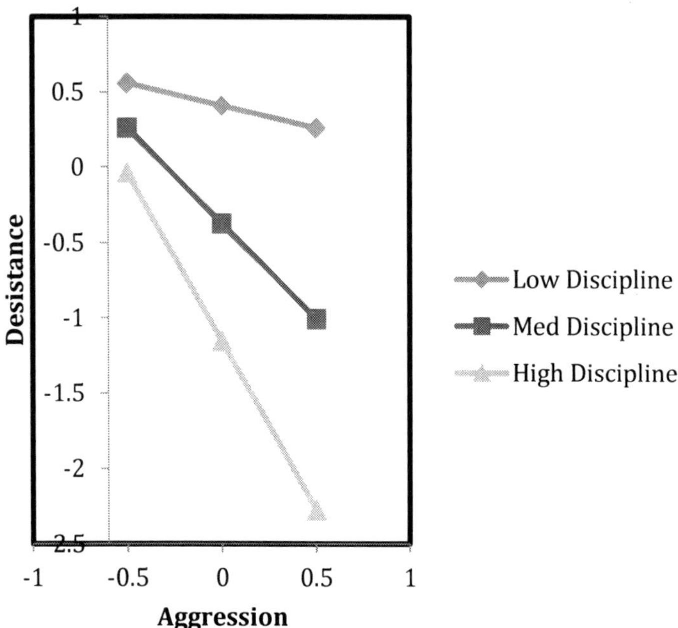

First, mother's antisocial behavior was tested as a mediator of the association between aggression and desistance. Mother's antisocial behavior was tested as a mediator of the association between aggression and desistance in an effort to understand to what extent parenting risk factors may explain individual risk for stable antisocial behavior. The model is depicted in Figure 2. As predicted, mother's antisocial behavior partially mediated the association between aggression and desistance. Aggression was significantly positively associated with mother's antisocial behavior (ß = .24 (.05), $p < .001$), and mother's antisocial behavior was significantly negatively associated with desistance (ß = -1.56 (.58), *p* < .001). Furthermore, aggression was significantly negatively associated with desistance without mother's antisocial behavior in the model (ß = -1.30 (.38), *p* < .001; however, aggression was a weaker predictor of desistance once mother's antisocial behavior was included in the model (ß = -1.00 (.41), p < .05). Results from a Sobel test (Preacher & Hayes, 2004) indicated that the mediation model was statistically significant (p<.05), confirming that mother's antisocial behavior partially mediated the association between aggression and desistance.

In addition, mother's antisocial behavior was tested as a mediator of the association between parental discipline and desistance. Mother's antisocial behavior was tested as a mediator of the association between parental discipline and desistance in an effort to understand to what extent mother's antisocial behavior may explain the influence of parenting practices on desistance. The model is depicted in Figure 3. Contrary to the hypotheses, parental discipline was not significantly negatively associated with mother's antisocial behavior. However, mother's antisocial behavior was significantly negatively associated with desistance (ß = -1.88 (.58), *p* < .001). Furthermore, parental discipline was significantly positively associated with desistance with and without mother's antisocial behavior in the model. Seeing that not all pathways in the model were statistically significant, a Sobel test was not necessary in this case. Therefore, mother's antisocial behavior was not found to mediate the association between parental discipline and desistance.

Finally, parental discipline was tested as a mediator of the association between exposure to violence and desistance. Parental discipline was tested as a mediator of the association between exposure to violence and desistance from crime in an effort to understand to what extent parenting may explain the impact of neighborhood factors on desistance. Given that there was not a significant interaction between parenting and neighborhood violence, mediation analyses were conducted to explore whether distal factors exert influence through their effects on proximal factors. The model is depicted in Figure 4. Exposure to violence was significantly negatively associated with parental discipline (ß = -0.14 (.08), $p < .05$ and parental discipline was significantly positively associated with desistance (ß = 2.78 (.79), $p < .001$. Furthermore, exposure to violence was significantly negatively associated with desistance with and without parental discipline in the model. Although all pathways in the model were statistically significant, results from Sobel test (Preacher & Hayes, 2004) indicated that the mediation merely approached significance ($p = .11$). As noted in the mediation results above, such a trend may be indicative of an important association that would be statistically significant if the analyses had greater power. Therefore, parental discipline is concluded to demonstrate a trend toward significance in partially mediating the association between exposure to neighborhood violence and desistance.

Figure 2. Mother's Antisocial Behavior as a Mediator of Aggression on Desistance

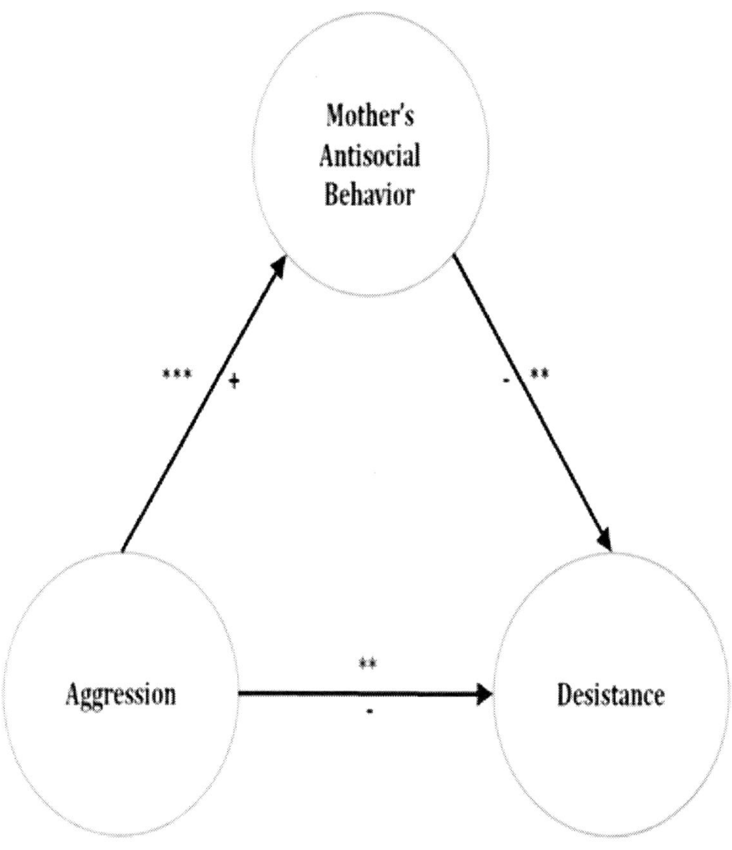

Figure 3. Mother's Antisocial Behavior as a Mediator of Parental Discipline on Desistance

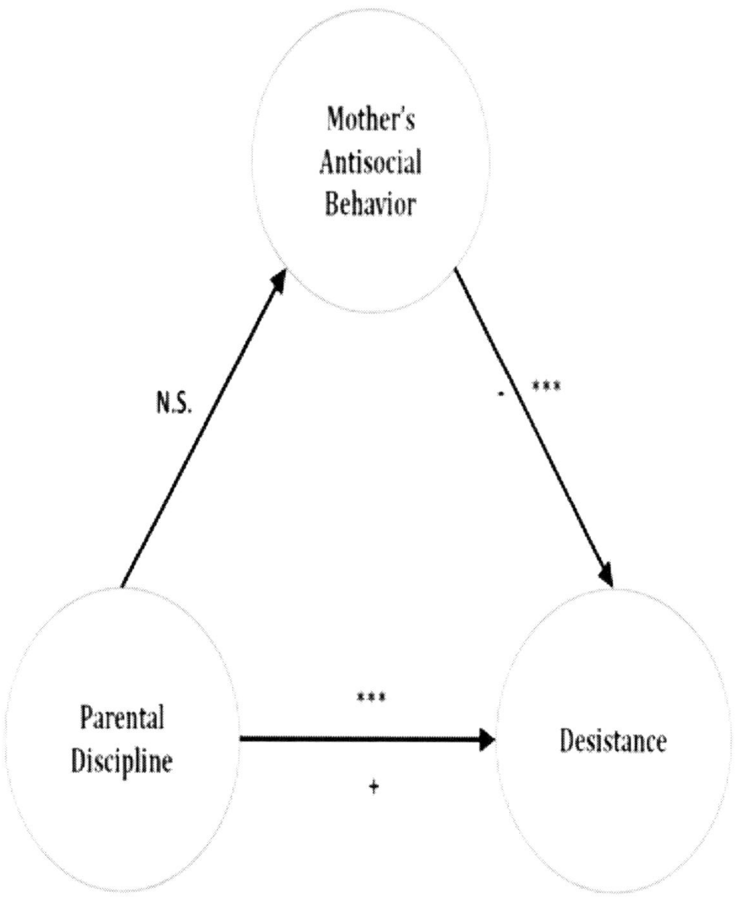

Figure 4. Parental Discipline as a Mediator of Exposure to Violence on Desistance

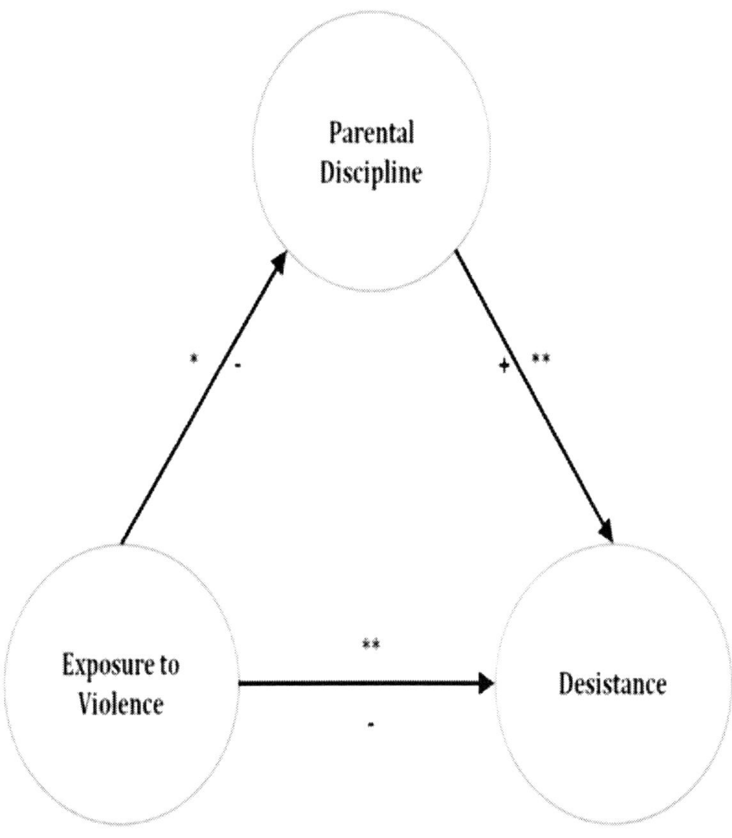

Chapter Five

Main Effects and Dynamic Processes Influencing Desistance

The present study deviates from more traditional literature on risk for the initiation and development of antisocial behavior. Instead, the present study answered several questions about the role of individual, family, and neighborhood factors during adolescence that contribute to the desistance process in early adulthood. Binary logistic regression models were used in order to identify mechanisms predicting persistence in and desistance from antisocial behavior over time, and analyses were conducted to investigate interactive processes between ecological variables that drive the desistance process. Additional models were also examined to delineate whether effects of aggression, discipline, and exposure to violence could be explained by additional underlying mechanisms.

The present study focused on a specialized sample of delinquent males selected from the Chicago Youth Development Study, therefore representing a high-risk, low-income, urban male sample. From a public health perspective, it is important to identify processes contributing to desistance in a population with high relative risk for delinquency. Young men commit a disproportionately large amount of total criminal offenses

(Rutter et al., 1998), which underscores the motivation for prioritizing such a population in the present study. In addition, poor African American males demonstrate less of a decline in violence in early adulthood compared to their Caucasian counterparts (Coie, 2004; Elliot, 1994), affirming the need to identify predictors of desistance in the present high-risk sample.

In sum, we found evidence for the roles of aggression, parental discipline, and exposure to neighborhood violence measured across adolescence in predicting desistance. Yet, aggression became a non-significant predictor after accounting for family and neighborhood factors, suggesting the possibility that risk from aggression could be explained by intervening variables. Furthermore, discipline moderated the association between aggression and desistance in aggressive youth. Mother's antisocial behavior partially explained the effect of aggression on desistance, and also moderated the effect of discipline, indicating that discipline practices no longer had a positive influence when mothers were highly antisocial. Collectively, the present findings underscore the importance of identifying both individual and contextual factors that promote desistance in low-income, urban males.

PREDICTIVE ECOLOGICAL FACTORS

<u>Individual Characteristics</u>
Contrary to previous findings on impulsivity being highly associated with later delinquency, impulsivity was not significantly associated with desistance, nor was there a significant interaction between impulsivity and aggression.

Consistent with the hypotheses and previous findings, aggression negatively predicted desistance from crime. In contrast to the belief that all externalizing behaviors make up a constellation of risk factors for persistent antisocial behavior, the present findings indicate differences between the predictive role of aggression compared with that of impulsivity. The high-risk nature of the present sample may have contributed to this finding, as baseline levels of behavioral problems were higher than would be found in a normative sample. Although impulsivity alone was not a predictor of desistance here, it may still be associated with other antisocial outcomes, with desistance measured at more proximal time intervals, or in more normative samples.

The present findings are consistent with research suggesting that persistent offenders can be identified early based on individual aggression (Moffitt, 1993), and extend those findings to predicting desistance. A plausible theoretical explanation is that children faced with high levels of contextual adversity and environmental stress experience consistently greater levels of arousal that manifest in aggressive behavior (Agnew, 1992). Transactions between aggressive youth and features of their environment may lead to persistent antisocial behavior, as prosocial skills decline and delinquency is reinforced over time (Moffitt, 2002). Our findings emphasize the importance of identifying individual and contextual factors that promote desistance in aggressive, inner-city youth.

<u>Family Processes</u>
Consistent with the hypotheses, parental discipline promoted later desistance. Discipline was the only

promotive factor found, and was the strongest predictor of desistance after all study variables were accounted for. Thus, discipline maintained significance after neighborhood factors were considered, emphasizing its impact embedded within an urban poor context. The promotive role of parenting was consistent with previous findings on family functioning and risk for violence (Gorman-Smith, et al., 1996, 2000, 2004). Our findings were also consistent with the association between harsh discipline and punitive parenting later offending (Patterson et al., 1992; Sampson & Laub, 1993). Our results also suggest that the role of discipline is robust across time. In addition, the present findings suggest that parenting may play a particularly salient role in urban poor families.

Contrary to the research hypotheses and previous findings, parental monitoring was not significantly associated with desistance. Youth living in disadvantaged, urban neighborhoods may be exposed to such high levels of environmental risk that parental monitoring is not enough to mitigate these negative circumstances, particularly when testing the impact of monitoring on later outcomes. Previous studies on inner-city families have found that positive family processes do not buffer the impact of neighborhood stress on antisocial behavior (Gorman-Smith et al., 1999; Gorman-Smith et al., 2004). Thus, youth in these communities may need larger efforts extending beyond the family to protect against such high community-level risk (Attar et al., 1994; Gorman-Smith, et al., 2004).

Research has traditionally focused on the role of parenting styles and practices in influencing delinquent outcomes (Patterson et al., 1989; Patterson et al., 2007); yet, less is known about the social transmission of parent antisocial behavior. Furthermore, although parent antisocial behavior has been shown to increase risk for delinquency, the mechanisms that explain this association remain unclear. Antisocial parenting characteristics may be transmitted to youth though genetic mechanisms, through parenting behaviors, or through behavioral modeling (Farrington & Welsh, 2007). We could not tease out the mechanisms through which mother's antisocial behavior impacts desistance in the present study. Yet, given the antisocial nature of our sample, we considered it important to examine the direct and indirect effect of mother's antisocial behavior on desistance.

Contrary to the research hypotheses, mother's antisocial behavior only approached significance in being negatively associated with desistance. As previously mentioned, there are several suggested explanations for the association between parent antisocial behavior and youth outcomes. Risk from mother's antisocial behavior may be transmitted indirectly through family poverty (Moffitt et al., 2002), harsh and coercive discipline (Patterson et al., 1992), and substance use (Robbins, 1998). Furthermore, antisocial behavior has been shown to be moderately heritable (Jaffee, Moffitt, Caspi, & Taylor, 2004); specifically, about forty to sixty percent of variance is typically accounted for by genetic factors (Rutter, Silberg, O'Connor, & Simonoff, 1999). Therefore, youth with antisocial mothers may be at particularly high risk for chronic delinquency as they are exposed to both genetic risk factors as well as corresponding environmental risk factors (Jaffee et al., 2004).

<u>Neighborhood Characteristics</u>
Contrary to the hypotheses that neighborhood social processes and resources would impact desistance, neither construct was statistically significant. Because participants lived in low-income, urban neighborhoods, it is possible that the variation of both neighborhood social processes and resources was too small to affect desistance. Tolan, Gorman-Smith, and Henry (2003) reported that in neighborhoods characterized most by concentrated poverty and crime, there was less reported neighborhood involvement, less felt support among neighbors, and a lower reported sense of neighborhood belonging. In addition, the presence of neighborhood social processes and resources may not have been sufficiently robust to influence long-term outcomes. The present findings do not discount the importance of considering the impact of similar neighborhood features on other antisocial outcomes, on declining delinquent behavior at more proximal time periods, or in less economically burdened communities.

Juvenile delinquency and adolescent substance use are higher in neighborhoods characterized by crime and violence (Gibson et al., 2009; Leventhal et al., 2000). Community violence exposure also increases risk for aggression and antisocial behavior, even controlling for previous levels of aggressive behavior (Gorman-Smith et al.,1999). We still have a limited understanding of how exposure to violence impacts youth, particularly considering both neighborhood and individual domains simultaneously (Buka et al., 2001).

Consistent with the study hypotheses, exposure to neighborhood violence had a significant negative impact on desistance, above and beyond individual and family characteristics. Although previous research has supported the role of families in mitigating neighborhood risk, the present findings stress the direct effect of exposure to violence on desistance. The present findings are consistent with previous work demonstrating the meaningful role of the neighborhood ecology for at-risk youth.

DYNAMIC PROCESSES IMPACTING DESISTANCE

Parent-child relationships influence the effect of environmental risk and protective factors, thus serving as a possible moderator; however, family relationships can also play a prominent role in explaining associations between social influences and adolescent outcomes, thus serving as a possible mediator (Grotevant, 1998). Based on previous literature demonstrating that parenting may function as both a moderator and mediator of individual and contextual factors, the present study examined how family factors operate in both roles in a high-risk sample.

Examining Protective Factors for Promoting Desistance
We explored whether the protective effect of parenting varied according to youth's aggression levels, and ultimately hypothesized that the predictive association between aggression and desistance would be differentially moderated by parental discipline. We hypothesized that parenting would have the strongest buffering effect among youth with the highest levels of aggression. Although there was as significant interaction between aggression and discipline, the direction of the association was not as hypothesized. Conversely, discipline was actually a risk factor for persistence in the highly aggressive participants.

On the other hand, discipline did not serve as a moderator for less aggressive youth in the sample, indicating a distinctive finding regarding the role of parents for aggressive, inner-city males.

There are several potential explanations for the complex nature of the interaction between aggression and discipline practices. Protective factors are complex, because risk to one youth may be protection to another. Subsequently, **the finding that discipline was positively related to desistance in the overall sample although negatively related to desistance for the aggressive youth illustrates the intricate process involved with promoting resiliency in particularly high-risk populations.** Another issue to consider is that most research on the role of parenting practices has focused on the impact of parenting during childhood on delinquency initiation and escalation during adolescence. In contrast, the present study examined the role of parent-child interactions during adolescence on outcomes in young adulthood. The detrimental influence of poor parenting for young children may also not apply for highly aggressive adolescent males. Furthermore, adolescent developmental research suggests that emotional autonomy may be a protective factor for teens (Fuhrman &Holmbeck, 1995), indicating that parent-youth closeness could be harmful during this complex developmental stage.

The present sample consists of inner-city, ethnic minority males who were selected for being at high-risk for the development of antisocial behavior. Therefore, the demographic background of the study participants could be relevant in explaining the unanticipated finding with parental discipline. There is also evidence that the cultural context of parenting moderates the impact of punishment;

specifically, it has been shown that punishment is associated with later aggression in European American families, although not in African American families (Deater-Deckard, Dodge, Bates, & Pettit, 1996). An explanation for the moderating role of ethnic group on the effect of discipline is that punitive parenting is more normative in African American families, thus being perceived by the child more positively than in European American families where this is often perceived by the child as rejection (Dodge, Coie, & Lynam, 2008).

In the present study, the discipline construct was measured such that positive scores indicated positive parenting practices and positive parent-child communication about rules and standards (see Methods chapter for details). Subsequently, a parent reporting harsh discipline practices would receive a low score on the discipline construct. Moreover, authoritarian parenting is characterized by a restrictive, punitive parenting style, correspondingly low in bidirectional communication and reciprocity (Baumrind, 1991). It has been proposed that because low-income, ethnic minority families often live in dangerous neighborhoods, authoritarian parenting may benefit such at-risk youth (Furstenberg, Cook, Eccles, Elder, Sameroff, 1999). Research on juvenile offenders has shown that indulgent parenting is strongly predictive of later delinquency, although authoritarian parenting was not (Steinberg, 2006); this finding suggests that authoritarian discipline may not be detrimental for many juvenile offenders. Consistently, it is possible that harsher parenting is more important for aggressive male youth; specifically, aggressive males might benefit from stricter parental discipline because they lack the abilities to inhibit their own risky behavior.

Another possible explanation for the unanticipated interaction finding is that there are salient aspects of parenting that were not captured with the discipline construct. The discipline construct may have captured some parenting practices and strategies without assessing more discrete aspects of the relationship, albeit equally important. Emotional support and warmth may not have been effectively captured, as discipline measures often capture firmness and consistency, while not measuring warmth (Steinberg, Blatt-Eisengart, & Cauffman, 2006). Parents who use harsh, inconsistent discipline practices while simultaneously providing emotional support may also be qualitatively different from those who employ punitive practices while offering little support or warmth to their sons.

The association between harsh discipline and aggressive behavior may be explained by whether disciplinary practices are executed in an emotionally controlled or uncontrolled manner (Chang, Schwarz, Dodge, & McBride- Chang, 2003). The association between aggression and delinquency is also sometimes buffered by parental warmth (Pagani, Japel, Vaillancourt, Tremblay,& Cote, 2008). Moderate amounts of parental discipline may also be beneficial for adolescents whose family relationships are positive (Adams & Laursen, 2007), suggesting that the influence of discipline might be particularly complex. Thus, there may be subtle aspects of the complex parent-adolescent relationship that determine how discipline affects antisocial behavior.

The prevalence of antisocial families in our sample may also have contributed to the nature of the interaction between aggression and discipline. The advocates of social learning approaches suggest that youth often model antisocial behavior seen in parents (Patterson et al., 1989), emphasizing the role of parental deviancy in predicting stable delinquency. Subsequently, close parent-child relationships may lead to an increased risk for antisocial persistence if youth model criminal behavior seen in their parents. Behavioral modeling may be particularly salient for aggressive youth, as they are already predisposed to persistent behavioral problems based on their individual characteristics. Dodge (2003) proposes that the developmental course of aggression is influenced by parenting styles that generally endorse deviant behavior. Parent-child closeness may actually be a risk factor for persistence in antisocial families.

As the present sample was selected for being at high-risk for antisocial behavior, participants are likely to live in family contexts characterized by such deviant behavior. Subsequently, parenting might be critically different in these homes than in normative populations. Encouraging close parent-child relationships may not necessarily be an effective prevention strategy for all families. When designing policies and programs aimed at reducing risk in the family context, parental involvement should not necessarily be assumed to be positive. Parents with aggressive boys might also require a more complex approach to family-based prevention than do normative samples, especially as antisocial behavior is known to to run in families (Farrington & Welsh, 2007).

<u>Underlying Mechanisms Driving Desistance</u>
After testing interactions,__ mediation models were examined to test whether there were other factors driving the main effects found. The first model was tested in an effort to explain the association between aggression and desistance, as aggression did not maintain statistical significance in the main effect models once family and neighborhood factors were accounted for. Therefore, mother's antisocial behavior was tested as a potential mediator of risk from aggression. In addition, mother's antisocial behavior was tested as a mediator of the association between discipline and desistance in an effort to decipher whether the impact of parental discipline was explained by the antisocial behavior of mothers in the sample. Finally, discipline was tested as a mediator of the association between exposure to neighborhood violence and desistance in an effort to understand whether neighborhood factors affect youth outcomes through their effect on proximal family processes.

The direct association between aggression and desistance was partially mediated by mother's antisocial behavior, verifying the important role of parent criminality in explaining individual risk pathways. Family systems theorists assert that parent-child interactions must be viewed in the broader family context (Minuchin, 1985), suggesting that the role of family factors must be considered entirely to understand individual psychosocial processes (Pagani et al., 2008). Furthermore, the association between aggression and mother's antisocial behavior might indicate an underlying genetic component; however, mother's antisocial behavior may also mediate the association between aggression and desistance through social contagion processes (Rutter, 1998). Genetics have been shown to play a larger role in determining persistent antisocial behavior compared with adolescent- limited behavior (Rutter et al., 1997). Moreover, parent-child relationship dynamics should be considered in the context of other family characteristics, in particular parent criminal behavior.

Investigating the mediating role of parent delinquency adds to the body of knowledge concerning how individual risk factors operate over time. The findings reported here suggest that risk for chronic antisocial behavior result from a convergence of both individual risk factors and characteristics of the youth's proximal social environment. Support for the significant mediating role of family factors might be found in social learning theories (Patterson et al., 1989), suggesting that aggressive behavior is modeled through social exchanges in the family ecology. It is unclear whether the mediating role of mother's antisocial behavior is more deeply explained by coercive exchanges, poor parent-child communication, behavioral modeling, or even by genetic mediation.

Mother's antisocial behavior was tested as a mediator of the association between discipline and desistance in order to better understand the dynamic functions of family factors. There is considerable evidence for the association between parent antisocial behavior and children's behavioral problems (Jaffee et al., 2004). A question that remains is whether parent criminality mediates the association between parenting practices and desistance. Mother's antisocial behavior was tested as a mediator of discipline, in order to identify whether the impact of parent-child interactions differ based on the antisocial behavior of the parent. Although mother's antisocial behavior was hypothesized to mediate the effect of discipline on desistance, the model was not statistically significant.

As discussed previously, close parent-child relationships may not be protective for youth raised in high-risk family environments. Therefore, youth who have close relationships to antisocial parents may be at greater risk for persistent delinquency, compared to youth from normative families or to youth who are more autonomous. Based on this rationale, mother's antisocial behavior was predicted to explain the complex role of parental discipline. However, as the mediation model tested was not statistically significant, additional post-hoc analyses were conducted to elucidate the role of mother's antisocial behavior in driving the effect of discipline on desistance. In order to compare aggression and discipline scores for participants with high and low mother's antisocial behavior, independent samples t-tests were conducted. T-tests were conducted to delineate whether mother's antisocial behavior played an underlying role in driving the moderating effect of discipline on risk from aggression.

Prior to conducting the t-test, participants were grouped into high and low categories for mother's antisocial behavior, based on whether they were above or below the mean for the variable's distribution. As shown in Tables 10 and 11, there was a significant difference in the aggression scores for the low mother's AB group ($\mu = 2.33$, $\partial = .47$), and the high mother's AB group ($\mu = 2.61$, $\partial = .50$; $t(194) = -3.98$, $p < .001$, two-tailed). The magnitude of the differences in the means was approximately one standard deviation (mean difference $= -.28$, *95% CI*: -.41 to -.14). However, there was not a significant difference in the parental discipline scores for the low and high mother's antisocial behavior groups. Based on the small sample size analyzed in the present study, significant differences between subgroups may indicate a trend of practical importance when seeking to understand the role of mother's antisocial behavior in the context of parenting aggressive youth. In conclusion, given that there was a significant interaction between aggression and discipline, the present t-test results suggest that mother's antisocial may have explained part of this association for the aggressive youths.

In order to further examine whether mother's antisocial behavior was playing a role in driving the direction of the interaction between aggression and discipline, post-hoc interactions were tested. Specifically, mother's antisocial behavior was tested as a moderator of the association between discipline and desistance in an effort to assess whether the effect of discipline varied based on the presence of mother's antisocial behavior. After centering the predictors and re-calculating the interaction terms, binary logistic regression was conducted to investigate associations with desistance. In addition, the interaction was probed by examining the association between discipline and desistance at high and low levels of mother's antisocial behavior.

The interaction results indicated that mother's antisocial behavior significantly moderated the effect of discipline on desistance. Furthermore, at low levels of mother's antisocial behavior, the association between discipline and desistance was positive and significant. Disciple was also a non-significant predictor of later desistance in the presence of high levels of mother's antisocial behavior. In other words, high levels of mother's antisocial behavior counteracted the positive effect of discipline on desistance. In order to further improve interpretation of the interaction, a graphical representation is displayed in Figure 5; the graph confirms the interpretation of the association between variables tested. For youth with highly antisocial mothers, discipline was not associated with desistance; in contrast, for youth with less antisocial mothers discipline did promote later desistance. As shown in Table 13, a cross-tabulation was also conducted to examine how many participants were represented in each group. Results demonstrated that there were a total of 82 participants who were classified as having medium and low levels of mother's antisocial behavior while also being exposed to high levels of parental discipline, representing approximately 42 % of the total sample.

Finally, discipline was promotive of desistance for youths with less antisocial mothers; however, discipline became a non-significant predictor in the presence of high levels of mother's antisocial behavior. Taken together, these several findings suggest the importance of considering the antisocial nature of mothers and their sons when examining the role of parenting. The interaction findings between discipline and mother's antisocial behavior could indicate an environmental effect, whereby the impact of parent-child dynamics varies based on the antisocial behavior of the parent. Social learning explanations suggest that in order to parent effectively, parents must be seen by their children as a source of positive emotion and warmth (Dodge et al., 2008). Antisocial parents may be viewed negatively by their children, thus reducing their ability to parent effectively.

In the final mediation model tested, discipline approached significance in mediating the association between exposure to neighborhood violence and desistance. There is evidence for neighborhood factors impacting developmental outcomes through their effects on the family unit (McLoyd, 1990). Previous studies have shown that family functioning protects youth who are exposed to neighborhood violence from engaging in violent behavior (Garbarino & Kostelny, 1992; Gorman-Smith et al., 2004). Family conflict has also been shown to mediate the association between economic disadvantage and adolescent aggression (Wadsworth & Compas, 2003), suggesting that broader contextual stressors may undermine parents' abilities to maintain positive relationships with their adolescents. Furthermore, youth exposed to high levels of neighborhood violence perpetrate less when they come from highly functioning families (Gorman-Smith et al., 2004). Finally, there is also evidence for a hierarchical theory of delinquency, with macrovariables affecting proximal family variables, family variables affecting child variables, and child variables affecting delinquent behavior (Loeber et al., 1998).

The present findings are consistent with those of Sheidow et al. (2001) who found that family functioning did not significantly mitigate risk from exposure to violence in highly impoverished inner-city communities. Consistent with the present findings, this suggests that in particularly high-risk communities, the family may play a less salient role in explaining risk from neighborhood effects. Furthermore, families have been shown to mediate the impact of stress on aggression in slightly lower-risk communities (Gorman-Smith & Tolan, 1998), emphasizing the importance of considering the broader environmental context when examining the effect of more proximal processes on antisocial behavior (Tolan, Guerra, & Kendall, 1995).

Altogether, post-hoc analyses demonstrated that mother's antisocial behavior partially mediated risk from aggression, and also significantly moderated the effect of parental discipline on desistance. Specifically, discipline was promotive of desistance for youths with less antisocial mothers; however, discipline became a non-significant promotive factor in the presence of high levels of mother's antisocial behavior. Finally, parental discipline approached significance in mediating risk from neighborhood violence exposure, demonstrating the need for a better understanding of the role of parenting operating in the context of macro-level factors. Family factors were found to have the most powerful effects on later desistance, both directly and indirectly. The present findings underscore the need to consider multiple aspects of the social context when seeking to understand the process of desistance in high-risk youth.

METHODOLOGICAL LIMITATIONS

As discussed, the present sample was pervasively high-risk, thus having considerably less statistical variation compared with a normative sample with regards to individual risk factors, exposure to environmental risk and in terms of delinquent outcomes. Additionally, the *non-offenders* were excluded in order to effectively analyze the desistance process. Decreasing the sample size subsequently reduced statistical power available to detect significant effects.

Additionally, the measurement of desistance was based on the theoretical conceptualization of desistance as the termination of antisocial behavior. Therefore, desistance was measured as a binary outcome variable, thus restricting the statistical range and potentially weakening associations found. Despite the limitations associated with a relatively small sample size and limited statistical power, the conceptualization of desistance provided a substantive reason for decreasing the sample size and for dichotomizing the outcome variable.

The present study relied on data from self-reports. A fundamental strength of self-report measures is that assessments can cover a wide range of environmental factors and of antisocial activities that are relevant to the present topic. Although measures were reliable, validity with external sources was not assessed. Specifically, self-reported data were not compared with data on police arrests or convictions. Discrepancies often exist between self-reported delinquency data and data from official crime records, specifically in ethnic minority populations (Huizinga & Elliot, 1986). The potential for systematic underreporting should be acknowledged as a limitation in the present study, as with other studies relying on self-reported delinquency data.

Finally, because of the selection criteria used in the present study, the findings may not be generalizable to normative populations and should therefore be interpreted with caution. Additionally, conclusions should not be drawn for females, or for racial groups other than African American and Latino youths.

PREVENTION IMPLICATIONS

The present findings suggest the need to create comprehensive, multi-level interventions with an emphasis on family-based strategies, particularly for disadvantaged urban youth. Although the association between aggression and desistance was powerful when tested alone, the predictive power of aggression was not significant once family and neighborhood factors were accounted for. On the other hand, although several factors were tested as potential moderators of risk from aggression, only parental discipline was significant in the present urban sample. Furthermore, discipline was not a significant protective factor for highly aggressive youth, suggesting the need to identify effective protective factors for this sub-group. As a small portion of the population is said to be responsible for the majority of crimes committed (Farrington & Welsh, 2007), and as aggression is the strongest behavioral risk factor for persistent criminal offending (Rutter et al., 1998), such youth should be the focus of selective prevention approaches designed to reduce propensity for offending. Moreover, prevention services should be provided to populations identified as being in most need of intervention. Target prevention strategies should aim to strengthen individual characteristics including social skills, prosocial behavior, emotional regulation, self-control, and other individual indicators of resilience in order to promote desistance in urban poor populations.

The salience of parental factors in predicting desistance has meaningful delinquency prevention implications for inner-city youth. Parental discipline significantly moderated the effects of aggression, and mother's antisocial behavior partially mediated the impact of aggression on desistance. Furthermore, discipline maintained significance in predicting desistance after neighborhood factors were accounted for, and became a non-significant promotive factor in the presence of high levels of mother's antisocial behavior. These findings confirm the importance of focusing intervention efforts in the family setting. The powerful role of proximal family processes suggests that programs designed to improve parent-child dynamics, and to reduce parental antisocial behavior may be beneficial to at-risk youth. Although parenting programs typically target families with young children, the present study shows that parents still play a crucial role during adolescence in determining adult behavior.

As exposure to violence during adolescence was significantly associated with risk for persistence, it is necessary to identify contextual and individual factors that mitigate such risk; this is of particular importance for urban youth living in crime-ridden neighborhoods. Structural neighborhood characteristics may facilitate violence in disadvantaged communities, subsequently making it difficult for adolescents to avoid violence exposure regardless of their individual propensity for crime (Leventhal & Brooks-Gunn, 2000). Therefore, prevention programs should be implemented to address multiple community risk factors in tandem with other ecological settings.

Because adversity is rarely a distinctive event and risk factors for delinquency tend to be cumulative, it is important to design multi-level interventions that target both the family and neighborhood settings. As desistance from crime was influenced by individual characteristics, family factors, and neighborhood conditions, interventions should be designed to address constellations of risk factors that span across multiple settings. In order for interventions to be most effective, they should ideally be suited to their target population; consistently, Rutter (1982) asserts that interventions should be designed for specific individuals under specific circumstances. As the present study focused on predicting desistance in a disadvantaged urban sample, implications can be drawn for similar populations living in chronic poverty. Low-income, inner-city populations are exposed to a multitude of associated risk factors, making it critical to focus public health prevention efforts in such communities.

Elucidating factors that influence the desistance process has meaningful policy implications for adjudicated youth. Identifying salient individual and contextual determinants of desistance should inform the design of rehabilitative interventions aimed at reducing recidivism in juveniles who are at-risk for incarceration. It is critically important to provide public mental health services to adjudicated youth targeting salient factors known to promote desistance. The present findings suggest that prevention and treatment efforts should devote attention to youth demonstrating early signs of aggression, notably those living in socially toxic neighborhoods and family contexts. Aggressive adolescent males exposed to environmental risk factors may be at particularly high-risk for persistent offending. Therefore, in order to improve developmental trajectories of such youth, resources should be devoted to understanding and promoting desistance in high-risk populations.

FUTURE RESEARCH

Although parental discipline was shown to buffer the association between aggression and desistance overall, research is needed to explain why the moderating effect was unique for the highly aggressive youth. Future research is needed to examine the transactional processes between parents and children that impact trajectories of antisocial behavior, particularly during the period of adolescence. In order to improve psychosocial outcomes of at-risk youth, it is critical to understand how dynamic interactions with parents influence the desistance process. Furthermore, it is likely that complex properties of parent-adolescent relationships affect pathways to desistance, emphasizing the need to develop a clear understanding of how to prevent parents from contributing to the escalation and persistence of antisocial behavior. Although there is evidence that discipline during adolescence is linked to poor psychosocial outcomes in young adulthood (Overbeek et al., 2007), this association might be highly variable based on the individual characteristics of youth and based on the broader family context.

Unfortunately, the present study did not find promising targets for interventions designed to reduce the impact of neighborhood risk on antisocial outcomes; however, the significant main effect of exposure to violence underscores the need for future studies to continue examining neighborhood risk processes. Although it is accepted that juvenile delinquency rates are highest in inner-city neighborhoods, specific neighborhood mechanisms driving this association remain poorly understood. Few neighborhood-based delinquency prevention interventions have also demonstrated sustainable outcomes, emphasizing the critical need to conduct future research on which macro-level factors are proximally related to delinquency. Although neighborhoods can affect youth through their mitigating effects on families, the present study did not find strong evidence for this pathway. Because there are issues of environmental selection when studying the influence of neighborhoods, it is challenging to differentiate between social selection and social causation processes. Furthermore, although antisocial families may select into high-crime neighborhoods, this hypothesized proclivity has yet to be tested empirically. Ultimately, interactions between individual, family, and neighborhood factors are likely to explain the complex pathways leading to desistance.

CONCLUSION

The results of the present study underscore the salient roles of aggression, parental discipline, mother's antisocial behavior, and exposure to neighborhood violence in predicting desistance from crime in an urban, minority, male sample. The present findings are consistent with an ecological view of antisocial behavior and additionally demonstrate how individual and contextual factors contribute to desistance in young adulthood. Parenting factors play a fundamental role in establishing trajectories of antisocial behavior and predicting desistance. Our findings also underscore the role of parenting in explaining and altering the effect of aggression. Therefore, interventions targeting parenting practices and family relationship dynamics may promote desistance in high-risk youth. The present findings also reinforce the importance of the neighborhood context in which families are embedded. Exposure to neighborhood violence is an important risk factor for persistence, and approached significance in being mediated by parental discipline.

This study deviated from the traditional literature focused on how risk factors during childhood affect antisocial behavior during adolescence. Instead, the present findings demonstrate the powerful role of ecological factors and processes during adolescence in predicting outcomes in young adulthood. Although developmental literature has traditionally focused on critical transitions for children, understanding delinquent involvement in emerging adulthood is of particular importance considering increasing societal demands on young adults. This study also focused on a sample of disadvantaged inner-city males, thus strengthening the understanding of a population at exceptionally high-risk for persistent crime. A unique contribution is made here by identifying subtle mechanisms that explain processes operating for antisocial youth. Understanding the dynamic nature of how risk and protective factors operate is necessary to promote desistance effectively. It remains critical to identify mechanisms that promote desistance in order to shape prevention programs and policies designed to reduce risk for chronic offending in disadvantaged youth.

Appendix

Table 8. Descriptive Statistics by Desistance Category: Desisters

Variable	N	Range	Minimum	Max	Mean (SD)
Mother's Education	67	6	1	7	4.03 (1.45)
Age	65	5	10	15	12.51 (1.21)
Aggression	75	2.25	1.44	3.68	2.29 (.47)
Impulsivity	75	2.37	1	3.37	2.00 (.49)
Monitoring	75	1.65	-1.13	.52	-.03 (.31)
Discipline	75	1.29	-.48	.82	.08 (.24)
Mother's AB	75	1.41	0	1.41	.68 (.32)
Social Processes	75	1.82	2.15	3.97	3.09 (.37)
Resources	75	2.02	.31	2.34	1.40 (.49)
Exp to Violence	75	1.11	0	1.11	.51 (.26)
Valid N	61				

Note. Max = Maximum, SD = Standard Deviation; Monitoring = Parental Monitoring, Discipline = Parental Discipline, Mother's AB = Mother's Antisocial Behavior, Social Processes = Neighborhood Social Processes, Resources = Neighborhood Resources, Exp to Violence = Exposure to Violence.

Table 9. Descriptive Statistics by Desistance Category: Persisters

	N	Range	Minimum	Max	Mean (SD)
Variable					
Mother's Education	49	6	1	7	3.88 (1.32)
Age	49	5	10	15	12.51 (1.18)
Aggression	60	2.44	1.54	3.98	2.51 (.48)
Impulsivity	60	1.78	1.22	3.00	2.08 (.42)
Monitoring	60	1.54	-1.06	.48	-.07 (.33)
Discipline	60	1.36	-.70	.67	.03 (.29)
Mother's AB	60	1.73	0	1.73	.80 (.39)
Social Processes	60	1.89	2.11	4.00	3.00 (.40)
Resources	60	1.71	.53	2.23	1.37 (.43)
Exposure to Violence	60	1.00	0	1.00	.55 (.23)
Valid N	43				

Note. Max = Maximum, SD = Standard Deviation; Monitoring = Parental Monitoring, Discipline = Parental Discipline, Mother's AB = Mother's Antisocial Behavior, Social Processes = Neighborhood Social Processes, Resources = Neighborhood Resources, Exp to Violence = Exposure to Violence.

Table 10. Summary of T-tests Based on Level of Mother's Antisocial Behavior

Variable	Mo AB Group	N	M	SD	SE Mean
Aggression	Low	109	2.33	.47	.05
	High	88	2.61	.50	.05
Discipline	Low	108	.03	.28	.03
	High	88	-.01	.26	.03

Note. Mo AB Group = Mother's Antisocial Behavior Group; M = Mean, SD = Standard Deviation, SE Mean = Standard Error of the Mean; Discipline = Parental Discipline.

Table 11. Independent Samples Test

Variable	t_{score}	df	F	p-value	M Diff	SE Diff	95% CI	
							Lower	Upper
Aggression	-3.98	194	.13	.00***	-.28	.07	-.41	-.14
Discipline	1.0	194	.13	.32	.39	.04	-.04	.12

Note. df = Degrees of Freedom, F = F-test; M Diff = Mean Difference; SE Diff = Standard Error Difference; 95% CI = 95% Confidence Interval; Discipline = Parental Discipline.
Equal variances were assumed when reporting results because Levene's Test p-values were over .05.
* = p < .05; ** = p < .01; *** = p < .001

Table 12. Cross Tabulation of Aggression x Parental Discipline

	Discipline			
	Low	Medium	High	Total
Aggression				
Low	22	65	12	99
High	9	72	16	97
Total	31	137	28	196

	Value	df	p-value (2-sided)
Pearson Chi-square	6.36	2	.042*
Likelihood Ratio	6.54	2	.038*
Linear by Linear Association	4.86	1	.027*
N	196		

Note. df = Degrees of Freedom.

Figure 5. Graph of Interaction between Parental Discipline and Mother's Antisocial Behavior

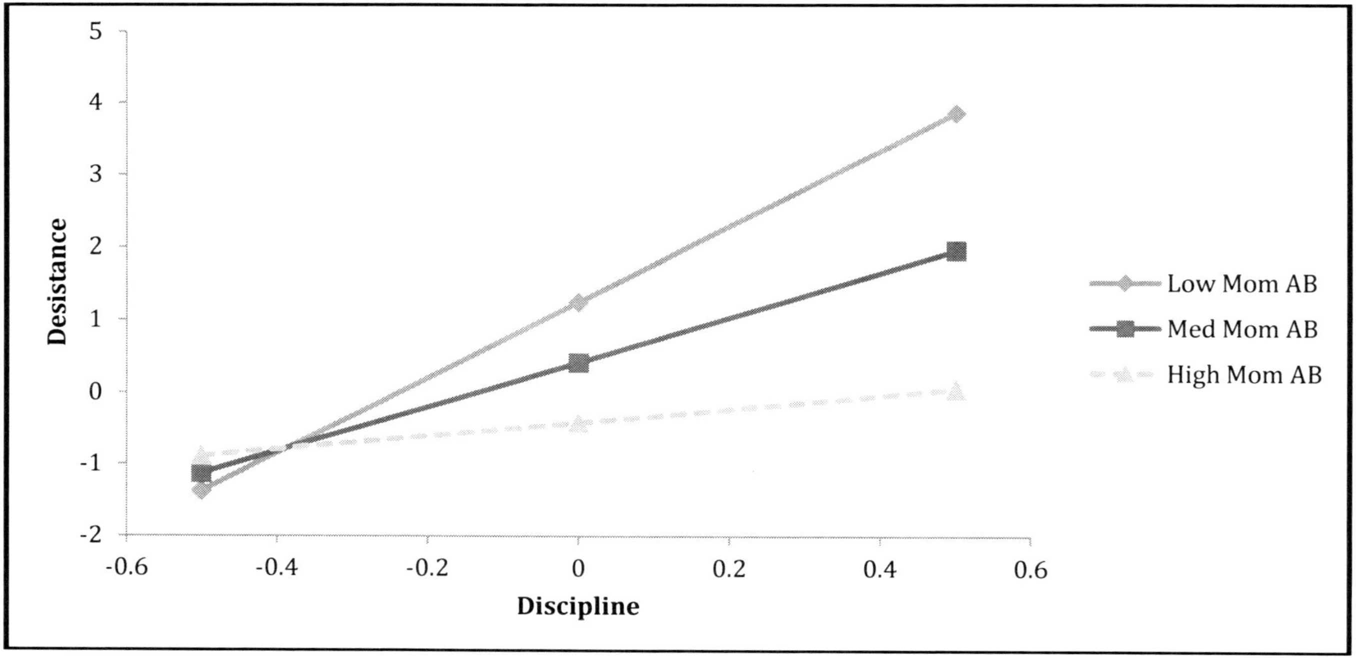

Table 13. Cross Tabulation of Parental Discipline x Mother's Antisocial Behavior

	Mother's Antisocial Behavior			
	Low	Medium	High	Total
Discipline				
Low	5	76	18	99
High	5	77	15	97
Total	10	153	33	196

	Value	df	p-value (2-sided)
Pearson Chi-square	.73	2	.69
Likelihood Ratio	.73	2	.69
Linear by Linear Association	.54	1	.46
N	194		

Note. df = Degrees of Freedom.

Bibliography

Achenbach, T.M. (1991). *Manual for the Child Behavior Checklist/ 4-18 and 1991 Profile*. Burlington: University of Vermont, Department of Psychiatry.

Adams, R.E., & Laursen, B. (2007). The correlates of conflict: Disagreement is not necessarily detrimental. *Journal of Family Psychology, 21*, 445-458.

Agnew, R. (1992). Foundations for a general strain theory of crime and delinquency. *Criminology, 30*, 47-47.

Aiken, L.S., & West, S.G. (1991). *Multiple Regression: Testing and Interpreting Interactions*. Newbury Park, VA: Sage.

Amato, P. R. (2001). Children of divorce in the 1990s: An updated of the Amato and Keith (1991) meta-analysis. *Journal of Family* Psychology, *15, 355*.

Azar, S. T. (2002).Parenting and Child Maltreatment. In M.H. Bornstein (Ed.), *Handbook of Parenting* (pp. 361-388). New Jersey: Lawrence Erlbaum Associates, Inc.

Baron, R.M., & Kenny, D.A. (1986). The moderator-mediator variable distinction in social psychological research: Conceptual, strategic, and statistical considerations. *Journal of Personality and Social Psychology, 51*, 1173-1182.

Baumeister, A.A., & Hawkins, M.F. (2001). Incoherence of neuroimaging studies in attention deficit/hyperactivity disorder. *Clinical Neuropharmacology, 24*, 2-10.

Baumrind, D. (1971). Current patterns of parental authority. *Developmental Psychology Monograph, 4,* 1-103.

Baumrind, D. (1973). The development of instrumental competence through socialization. *Minnesota Symposium on Child Psychology*: Vol. 7 (pp. 3-46). Minneapolis: University of Minnesota Press.

Baumrind, D. (1991). Parenting styles and adolescent development. In M.H. Bornstein (Ed.) *Handbook of Parenting* (pp.149-173). New Jersey: Lawrence Erlbaum Associates, Inc.

Belsky, J., Jaffee, S., Hseih, K.H., Silva, P.A. (2001). Child-rearing antecedents of intergenerational relations in young adulthood: A prospective study. *Developmental Psychology, 37,* 801-813.

Bor, W., McGee, T.R., & Fagan, A.A. (2004). Early risk factors for adolescent antisocial behaviour: An Australian longitudinal study. *Australian & New Zealand Journal of Psychiatry, 38,* 365-372.

Bornstein, M.H., & Cote, L.R. (2006). Parenting cognitions and practices in the acculturative process. In M.H. Bornstein & L.R. Cote (Eds.), *Acculturation and parent-child relationships: Measurement and development* (pp. 173-196). Mahwah, NJ: Lawrence Erlbaum.

Brady, S.S., Gorman-Smith, D., Henry, D.B., Tolan, P.H. (2008). Adaptive coping reduces the impact of community violence exposure on violent behavior among African American and Latino male adolescents. *Journal of Abnormal Child Psychology*, 36, 105-115.

Broidy, L. M., Nagin, D. S., Tremblay, R. E., Bates, J. E., Brame, B., Dodge, K .A., et al. (2003). Developmental trajectories of childhood disruptive behaviors and adolescent delinquency: A six-site, cross-national study. *Developmental Psychology, 39,* 222-245.

Bronfenbrenner, U. (1979). *The ecology of human development: Experiments by nature and design.* Cambridge: Harvard University Press.

Bronfenbrenner, U. (1994). Ecological models of human development. In T. Husen & T. N. Postlethwaite (Eds.), *The International Encyclopedia of Education* (2nd ed., pp. 1643-1647). New York: Elsevier Science.

Brooks-Gunn, J., Duncan, G., & Aber, J. (1997).*Neighborhood Poverty: Context and Consequences for Children.* New York: Russell Sage.

Browning, C. R., Burrington, L., Leventhal, T., & Brooks-Gunn, J. (2008). Neighborhood   structural inequality, collective efficacy, and sexual risk behavior among urban youth. *Journal of Health and Social Behavior,* 49, 269-285.

Buka, S.L., Stichick, T.L., Birdthistle, I., & Earls, F.J. (2001). Youth exposure to violence: Prevalence, risks, and consequences. *American Journal of Orthopsychiatry, 71*, 298- 310.

Campa, M.I., Bradshaw, C.P., Eckenrode, J.E., & Zielinski, D.Z. (2008). Examining patterns of problem behavior in relation to thriving and precocious behavior in late adolescence. *Journal of Youth and Adolescence, 37,* 627-640.

Capaldi, D., & Patterson, G. (1994). Interrelated influences of contextual factors on antisocial behavior in childhood and adolescence for males. In B. Hankin & J. Abela (Eds.), *Development of Psychopathology.* Thousand Oaks: Sage Publications.

Capaldi, D., & Patterson, G. (1996). Can violent offenders be distinguished from frequent offenders: Predictions from childhood to adolescence. *Journal of Research in Crime and Delinquency, 33,* 206-231.

Caspi, A. (2000). The child is father of the man: Personality continuities from childhood to adulthood. *Journal of Personality and Social Psychology, 78,* 158-172.

Caspi, A., & Moffitt, T.E. (1992). The continuity of maladaptive behavior: From description to understanding in the study of antisocial behavior. In D. Cicchetti & D. Cohen (Eds.), *Manual of Developmental Psychology.* New York: Wiley.

Catalano, R. F., & Hawkins, J. D. (1996). The social development model: A theory of antisocial behavior. In J. D. Hawkins (Ed.), D*elinquency and Crime: Current theories* (pp. 149-197). New York: Cambridge University Press.

Chang, L., Schwarz, D., Dodge, K., & McBride-Chang, C. (2003). Harsh parenting in relation to child emotion regulation and aggression. *Journal of Family Psychology, 17,* 598-606.

Chung, H., & Steinberg, L. (2006). Neighborhood, parenting, and peer influences on antisocial behavior among serious juvenile offenders. *Developmental Psychology, 42,* 319-331.

Cleveland, M.J., Gibbons, F.X., Gerrard, M., Pomery, E.A. & Brody, G.H. (2005). The impact of parenting on risk cognitions and risk behavior: A study of mediation and moderation in a panel of African American adolescents. *Child Development, 76,*900-916.

Cohen, J. (1987). Statistical Power Analysis for the Behavioral Sciences. Hillsdale, NJ: Lawrence Erlbaum.

Cohen, J., Cohen, P., West, S.G., & Aiken, L.S. (2003). *Applied Multiple Regression/Correlation Analysis for the Behavioral Sciences*. Mahwah, NJ: Lawrence Erlbaum Associates, Publishers.

Coie, J.D. (2004). The impact of negative social experiences on the development of antisocial behavior. In J.B. Kupersmidt & K.A. Dodge (Eds.), *Children's Peer Relations: From Development to Intervention* (pp. 243-267). Washington, DC: American Psychological Association.

Coie, J.D., & Dodge, K.A. (1998). Aggression and Antisocial Behavior. In W. Damon & N. Eisenberg (Eds.), *Handbook of Child Psychology: Social, Emotional, and Personality Development*. New York: Wiley.

Colder, C., Mott, J., Levy, S., & Flay, B. (2000). The relation of perceived neighborhood danger to childhood aggression: A test of mediating mechanisms. *American Journal of Community Psychology, 28*, 83-103.

Coleman, J.S. (1990). *Foundations of Social Theory*. Belnap Press of Harvard University Press: Cambridge, MA.

Collins, W., & Laursen, B. (2004). Parent-adolescent relationships and influences. In *R.M. Lerner & L.D. Steinberg (Eds.), Handbook* of Adolescent Psychology. Hoboken, NJ: John Wiley & Sons.

Collins, W. A., & Madsen, S. D. (2002). Developmental change in parenting interactions. In L. Kuczynski (Ed.), *Handbook of Dynamics in Parent-Child Relations*. Thousand Oaks, CA: Sage Publications.

Conger, R.D., Patterson, G.R., & Ge, X. (1995). It takes two to replicate: A mediational model for the impact of parents' stress on adolescent adjustment. *Child Development, 66*, 80-97.

Cox, D.R., & Snell, E.J. (1989). *Analysis of Binary Data, 2nd Edition*. London: Chapman and Hall.

Darling, N., & Steinberg, L. (1993). Parenting style as context: An integrative model. *Psychological Bulletin, 113*, 487.

Davidson, R.J., Putnam, K.M., & Larson, C.L. (2000). Dysfunction in the neural circuitry of emotion regulation: A possible prelude to violence. *Science, 289*, 591-594.

Deater-Deckard, K., & Dodge, K.A. (1997). Externalizing behavior problems and discipline revisited: Nonlinear effects and variation by culture, context, and gender. *Psychological Inquiry, 8*, 161-175.

Deater-Deckard, K., Dodge, K.A., Bates, J.E., & Pettit, G.S. (1996). Physical discipline among African-American and European- American mothers: Links to children's externalizing behaviors. *Developmental Psychology, 32*, 1065- 1072.

Dishion, T.J., Capaldi, D.M., & Yoerger, K. (1999). Middle childhood antecedents to progressions in male adolescent substance use: An ecological analysis of risk and protection. *Journal of Adolescent Research, 14*, 175-205.

Dishion, T. J., & McMahon, R. J. (1998). Parental monitoring and the prevention of child and adolescent problem behavior: A conceptual and empirical formulation. *Clinical Child and Family Psychology Review, 1*, 61–75.

Dishion, T. J., & Patterson, G. R. (2006). The development and ecology of antisocial behavior. In D. Cicchetti & D.

J. Cohen (Eds.), *Developmental Psychopathology*. Vol. 3: Risk, disorder, and adaptation (pp. 503–541). New York: Wiley.

Dodge, K.A., Bates, J.E., & Pettit, G.S. (1990). Mechanisms in the cycle of violence. *Science, 250,* 1678- 1683.

Dodge, K.A., Coie, J., & Lynam, D. (2008). Aggression and antisocial behavior in youth. In W. Damon & R. Lerner (Eds.), *Child and Adolescent Development: An Advanced Course* (pp. 437-472). New Jersey: John Wiley & Sons.

Dodge, K.A., & Pettit, G.S. (2003). A biopsychosocial model of the development of chronic conduct problems in adolescence. *Developmental Psychology, 39,* 349-371.

Duncan, G., Brooks-Gunn, J., & Klebanov, P. (1994). Economic deprivation and early childhood development. *Child Development*, *65*, 296-318.

Earls, F.J., Brooks-Gunn, J., Raudenbush, S.W., & Sampson, R.J. (2002). *Project of Human Development in Chicago Neighborhoods (PHDCN): Conflict Tactics for Parent and Child, Wave 1, 1994-1997.* Ann Arbor, MI: Inter-university Consortium for Political and Social Research. Doi: 10.3886/ ICPSR13584.

Elliot, D.S. (1994). Serious violent offenders: Onset, developmental course, and termination: The American Society of Criminology 1993 Presidential Address. *Criminology, 32*, 1-21.

Elliot, D.S., Dunford, F.W., & Huizinga, D. (1987). The identification and prediction of career offenders utilizing self-reported and official data. In G.W. Albee & J.M. Joffee (Series Eds.), *Primary Prevention of*

Psychopathology, Volume 10. Newbury Park, CA: Sage.

Elliot, D.S., Wilson, W.J., Huizinga, D., Sampson, R.J., Elliot, A., & Rankin, B. (1996). The effects of neighborhood disadvantage on adolescent development. *Journal of Research in Crime and Delinquency, 33*, 389-426.

Eron, L., Huesmann, L., & Zelli, A. (1991). The role of parental variables in the learning of aggression. In D. Pepler, & K. Rubin, (Eds.). *The Development and Treatment of Childhood Aggression.* Hillsdale, NJ: Lawrence Erlbaum.

Farrall, S., & Calverley, A. (2006). *Understanding Desistance from Crime*. London: Open University Press.

Farrington, D. (1992). Juvenile delinquency. In Coleman, J. (Ed.), *The School Years*, 2nd Edition. London: Routledge.

Farrington, D., Barnes, G., & Lambert, S. (1996). The concentration of offending in families. *Legal and Criminological Psychology, 1,* 47-63.

Farrington, D.P., Jolliffe, D., Loeber, R., Stouthamer-Loeber, M., & Kalb, L.M. (2001). The concentration of offenders in families, and family criminality in the prediction of boys' delinquency. *Journal of Adolescence, 24,* 579-596.

Farrington, D.P., Loeber, R., & Stouthhamer-Loeber, M. (2003). How can the relationship between race and violence be explained? In D.F. Hawkins (Ed.), *Violent Crime: Assessing Race and Ethnic Differences* (pp. 213-237). Cambridge, UK: Cambridge University Press.

Farrington, D., & Welsh, B. (2007). *Saving Children from a Life of Crime*. New York: Oxford University Press.

Fergusson, D.M., Horwood, L.J., & Ridder, E.M. (2005). Tests of causal linkages between cannabis use and psychotic symptoms. *Addiction*, 100, 354-366.

Fuhrman, T., & Holmbeck, G.N. (1995). A contextual-moderator analysis of emotional autonomy and adjustment in adolescence. *Child Development, 66,* 793-811.

Furstenberg, F.F., Cook, T.D., Eccles, J., Elder, G.H., & Sameroff, A. (1999). *Managing to Make It: Urban Families and Adolescent Success.* Chicago: University of Chicago.

Gardner, M. (2006). *Testing a New Typology of Juvenile Offenders: An Attempt to Differentiate Early and Late Onset Offenders.* (Doctoral dissertation, Temple University, 2006). Proquest Dissertation & Theses 3211870.

Gardner, F., Shaw, D.S., Dishion, T.J., Burton, J., & Supplee, L. (2007). Randomized prevention trial for early conduct problems: Effects on proactive parenting and links to toddler disruptive behavior. *Journal of Family Psychology, 21,* 398-406.

Garbarino, J., & Kostelny, K. (1992). Child maltreatment as a community problem. *International Journal of Child Abuse and Neglect, 16,* 455- 464.

Garbarino, J., Kostelny, K., & Dubrow, N. (1991). *No Place to be a Child: Growing up in a War Zone*. Lexington Books: Lexington, MA.

Ge, X., Brody, G.H., Conger, R.D., Simons, R.L., & Murry, V. (2002). Contextual amplification of pubertal transition effects on deviant peer affiliation and externalizing behavior among African American children. *Developmental Psychology, 38*, 42-54.

Gershoff, E.T. (2002). Corporal punishment by parents and associated child behaviors and experiences: A meta-analytic and theoretical review. *Psychological Bulletin, 128,* 539-579.

Gibson, C.L., Morris, S.Z., & Beaver, K.M. (2009). Secondary exposure to violence during childhood and adolescence: Does neighborhood context matter? *Justice Quarterly, 26*, 30-57.

Gorman-Smith, D., Henry, D.B., & Tolan, P.H. (2004). Exposure to community violence and violence perpetration: The protective effects of family functioning. *Journal of Clinical Child and Adolescent Psychology, 33,* 439-449

Gorman-Smith, D., & Tolan, P. (1998). The role of exposure to community violence and developmental problems among inner-city youth. *Development and Psychopathology, 10*, 101-116.

Gorman-Smith, D., Tolan, P.H., & Henry, D. (1999). The relation of community and family to risk among urban-poor adolescents. In P. Cohen & C. Slomkowski (Eds.), *Historical and Geographical Influences on Psychopathology* (pp. 349-367). Mahwah, NJ: Lawrence Erlbaum.

Gorman-Smith, D., Tolan, P.H., & Henry, D. (2000). A developmental-ecological model of the relation of family functioning to patterns of delinquency. *Journal of Quantitative Criminology, 16,* 169- 198.

Gorman-Smith, D., Tolan, P., Loeber, R., & Henry, D. (1998). Relation of family problems to patterns of delinquent involvement among urban youth. *Journal of Abnormal Child Psychology, 26*, 319-333.

Gorman-Smith, D., Tolan, P.H., Sheidow, A.J., & Henry, D.B. (2001). Partner violence and street violence among urban adolescents: Do the same family factors relate? *Journal of Research on Adolescence, 11*, 273-295.

Gorman-Smith, D., Tolan, P., Zelli, A., & Huesmann, L. (1996). The relation of family functioning to violence among inner-city minority youths. *Journal of Family Psychology, 10*, 115-129.

Gottfredson, M.R., & Hirschi, T. (1990). *A General Theory of Crime*. Stanford, CA: Stanford University Press.

Gottfredson, D., McNeil, R., & Gottfredson, G. (1991). Social area influences on delinquency: A multi-level analysis. *Journal of Research in Crime and Delinquency, 28*, 197-226.

Griffin, K.W., Botvin, G.J., Scheier, L.M., Diaz, T., & Miller, N.L. (2000). Parenting practices as predictors of substance use, delinquency, and aggression among urban minority youth: Moderating effects of family structure and gender. *Psychology of Addictive Behaviors, 14*, 174-184.

Guerra, N. G., Huesmann, L. R., Tolan, P. H., Van Acker, R., & Eron, L. D. (1995). Stressful events and individual beliefs as correlates of economic disadvantage and aggression among urban children. *Journal of Consulting and Clinical Psychology, 63*, 518-528.

Guerra, N., Williams, K, Tolan, P., & Modecki, K.L. (2008). Theoretical and research advances in understanding youth crime. In R.D. Hoge, N. Guerra,

& P. Boxer (Eds.), *The Juvenile Offender: Treatment Approaches*. New York: Guilford Press.

Hart, C. H., Nelson, D.A., Robinson, C. D., Olsen, S. F., & McNeilly-Choque, M. K. (1998). Overt and relational aggression in Russian nursery-school-age children: Parenting style and marital linkages. *Developmental Psychology, 34*, 687-697.

Hawkins, J., Arthur, M., & Catalano, R. (1995). Preventing substance abuse. In M. Tonry & D. Farrington (Eds.), *Crime and Justice: Building a Safer Society: Strategic Approaches to Crime Prevention*. Chicago: University of Chicago Press.

Henggeler, S. W., & Borduin, C. M. (1990). Family Therapy and Beyond: A Multisystemic Approach to Treating the Behavior Problems of Children and Adolescents. Pacific Grove, CA: Brooks/Cole Publishing Company.

Henry, D.B., Tolan, P.H., & Gorman-Smith, D. (2001). Longitudinal family and peer group effects on violent and non-violent delinquency. *Journal of Child Clinical Psychology, 30*, 172-186.

Hirshi, T.,& Gottfredson, M. (1983). Age and the explanation of crime. *American Journal of Sociology, 89*, 552-584.

Huesmann, L. R. and Eron, L. D. (1984). Cognitive processes and the persistence of aggressive behavior. *Aggressive Behavior, 10*, 243-251.

Huizinga, D., &Elliot, D.S. (1986). Reassessing the reliability and validity of self-report delinquency measures. *Journal of Quantitative Criminology, 2*, 293-327.

Huizinga, D., & Jakob-Chien, C. (1998). The contemporaneous co-occurrence of serious and violent juvenile offending and other problem behaviors. In R. Loeber & D.P. Farrington (Eds.), *Serious and violent juvenile offenders: Risk factors and successful interventions.* Sage Publications: Beverly Hills.

Ingoldsby, E., Shaw, D.S., Winslow, E., Schonberg, M., Gilliom, M., & Criss, M. (2006). Neighborhood disadvantage, parent-child conflict, neighborhood peer relationships, and early antisocial behavior problem trajectories. *Journal of Abnormal Child Psychology, 34,* 303-331.

Jaffee, S., Caspi, A., Moffitt, T.E., Taylor, A., Dickson, N. (2001). Predicting early fatherhood and whether young fathers live with their children: Prospective findings and policy reconsiderations. *Journal of Child Psychology and Psychiatry, 42,* 803-815.

Jaffee, S.R., Caspi, A., Moffitt, T.E., & Taylor, A. (2004). Physical maltreatment victim to antisocial child: Evidence of an environmentally mediated process. *Journal of Abnormal Psychology, 113,* 44-55.

Jeglum-Bartusch, D.R., Lynam, D.R., Moffitt, T.E., and Silva, P.A. (1997). Is age important? Testing a general versus a developmental theory of antisocial behavior. *Criminology, 35*: 13-48.

Jencks, C., & Mayer, S. E. (1990). The social consequences of growing up in a poor neighborhood. In L. E. Lynn, Jr. & M.G.H. McGeary (Eds.*), Inner-City Poverty in the United States* (pp. 111-186). Washington, DC: National Academy Press.

Kazemian, L. & Farrington, D. P. (2005). Comparing the validity of prospective, retrospective and official onset for different offending categories. *Journal of Quantitative Criminology, 21,* 127-147.

Kerr, M., & Stattin, H. (2000). What parents know, how they know it, and several forms of adolescent adjustment: Further support for a reinterpretation of monitoring. *Developmental Psychology, 36,* 366 – 380.

Kohen, D.E., Leventhal, T., Dahinten, V.S., & McIntosh, C.N. (2008). Neighborhood disadvantage: Pathways for effects for young children. *Child Development, 79,* 156-169.

Krivo, L.J., & Peterson, R.D. (1996). Extremely disadvantaged neighborhoods and urban crime. *Social Forces, 75,* 619-650.

Lahey, B., Miller, T., Gordon, R., & Riley, A. (1999). Developmental epidemiology of the disruptive behavior disorders. In B. Hankin & J. Abela (Eds.), *Development of Psychopathology.* Thousand Oaks: Sage Publications.

Lahey, B., Waldman, I., and McBurnett, K. (1999). The development of antisocial behavior: An integrative causal model. *Journal of Child Psychology and Psychiatry, 40,* 669-682.

Lahey, B., Schwab-Stone, M., Goodman, S., Waldman, I., Camino, G., Rathouz, P., et al. (2000). Age and gender differences in oppositional behavior and conduct problems: A cross-sectional household study of middle childhood and adolescents. *Journal of Abnormal Psychology, 109,* 488-503.

Lansford, J.E., Chang, E., Dodge, K.A., Malone, P.S., Oburu, P., & Palmerus, K. et al. (2005). Physical discipline and children's adjustment: Cultural normativeness as a moderator. *Child Development, 76,* 1234-1246.

Laub, J.H., Nagin, D.S., & Sampson, R.J. (1998). Trajectories of change in criminal offending: Good marriages and the desistance process. *American Sociological Review, 63*, 225-238.

Laub, J.H., & Sampson, R.J. (2001). Understanding desistance from crime. *Crime and Justice, 28,* 1-69.

Law, J.H., & Barber, B.K. (2007). Neighborhood conditions, parenting, and adolescent functioning. *Journal of Human Behavior in the Social Environment, 14,* 91-118.

Leventhal, T., & Brooks-Gunn, J. (2000). The neighborhoods they live in: The effects of neighborhood residence on child and adolescent outcomes. *Psychological Bulletin, 126,* 309-337.

Lipsey, M.W., & Derzon, J.H. (1999). Predictors of violent or serious delinquency in adolescence and early adulthood: A synthesis of longitudinal research. In R. Loeber & D.P Farrington (Eds.), *Serious and Violent Juvenile Offenders: Risk Factors and Successful Interventions* (pp. 86-105). Thousand Oaks: Sage Publications.

Loeber, R., Farrington, D.P., Stouthamer-Loeber, M., & White, H.R. (2008). *Violence and Serious Theft: Development and Prediction from Childhood to Adulthood.* New York, NY: Routledge.

Loeber, R., & Farrington, D.P. (2000) Young children who commit crime: Epidemiology, developmental origins, risk factors, early interventions and policy implications. *Development and Psychopathology, 12,* 737-762.

Loeber, R., & Hay, D.F. (1996). Key issues in the development of aggression and violence from childhood to early adulthood. *Annual Review of Psychology, 48,* 371-410.

Loeber, R., & Stouthamer-Loeber, M. (1998). The development of juvenile aggression and violence: Some common misconceptions and controversies. *American Psychologist, 53,* 242- 259.

Loeber, R., Stouthamer-Loeber, M., Van Kammen, W.B., & Farrington, D.P. (1991). Initiation, escalation, and desistance in juvenile offending and their correlates. *Journal of Criminal Law and Criminology, 82,* 36-82.

Loeber, R., Wung, P., Keenan, K., Giroux, B., Stouthamer-Loeber, M., Van Kammen, W.B., & Maughan, B. (1993). Developmental pathways in disruptive child behavior. *Development and Psychopathology, 5,* 103-133.

Lösel, L., & Bender, D. (2003). Protective factors and resilience. In: D.P. Farrington & J.W. Coid (Eds.), *Early Prevention of Adult Antisocial Behaviour* (pp. 130-204). Cambridge University Press: Cambridge.

Luthar, S. S., & Goldstein, A. (2004). Children's exposure to community violence: Implications for understanding risk and resilience. *Journal of Clinical Child and Adolescent Psychology, 33,* 499-505.

Luthar, S. S., & Zigler, E. (1991). Vulnerability and competence: A review of research on resilience in childhood. *American Journal of Orthopsychiatry, 61,* 6-22

Lynam, D., Moffitt, T., & Stouthamer- Loeber, M.(1993). Explaining the relation between IQ and delinquency: Class, race, test motivation, school failure, or self-control? *Journal of Abnormal Psychology, 102,* 187-196.

Lynam, D.R., Loeber, R., & Stouthamer-Loeber, M. (2000). The interaction between impulsivity and neighborhood context on offending: The effects of impulsivity are stronger in poorer neighborhoods. *Journal of Abnormal Psychology, 109,* 563-574.

Lynch, M., & Cicchetti, D. (1998). An ecological-transactional analysis of children and contexts: The longitudinal interplay among child maltreatment, community violence, and children's symptomatology. *Development and Psychopathology, 10,* 235-257.

Maruna, S. (1998*). Redeeming One's Self: How Reformed Ex-Offenders Make Sense of Their Lives*, Doctor of Philosophy Dissertation, Northwestern University.

Mason, C.A., Cauce, A.M., Gonzales, N., & Hiraga, Y. (1996). Neither too sweet nor too sour: Problem peers, maternal control, and problem behavior in African American adolescents. *Child Development, 67,* 2115–2130.

Masten, A., & Shaffer, A. (2007). How Families Matter in Child Development: Reflections from Research on Risk and Resilience. In A. Clarke-Stewart & J. Dunn (Eds*.), Families Count.* New York: Cambridge University Press.

McCarthy, B., & Hagan, J. (2001). When crime pays: Capital, competence, and criminal success. *Social Forces, 79,* 1035-1060.

McLoyd, V. (1990). The impact of economic hardship on black families and children: Psychological distress, parenting and socioemotional development. *Child Development, 61,* 311-346.

McLoyd, V.C. (1998). Socioeconomic disadvantage and child development. *American Psychologist, 53,* 185-204.

McLoyd, V.C., Kaplan, R., Purtell, K.M., Bagley, E., Hardaway, C.R., & Smalls, C. (2009). Poverty and socioeconomic disadvantage in adolescence (pp. 444-491). In R.M. Lerner & L. Steinberg (Eds.), *Handbook of Adolescent Psychology: Contextual Influences on Adolescent Development* (3rd Edition). New Jersey: John Wiley & Sons, Inc.

Miech, R., Caspi, A., Moffitt, T., Wright, B., & Silva, P. (1999). Low socioeconomic status and mental disorders: A longitudinal study of selection and causation during young adulthood. *American Journal of Sociology, 104,* 1096-1131.

Moffitt, T.E. (1990). The neuropsychology of juvenile delinquency: A critical review. In M. Tonry, & N. Morris (Eds.), *Crime and Justice*: Volume 12. Chicago: University of Chicago Press.

Moffitt, T.E. (1993). Adolescence-limited and life-course persistent antisocial behavior: A developmental taxonomy. *Psychological Review, 100,* 674- 701.

Moffitt, T.E. (2006). Life-course persistent versus adolescence-limited antisocial behavior. In D. Cicchetti & D. J. Cohen (Eds.), *Developmental Psychopathology: Vol. 3 (2nd Ed.). Risk, Disorder, and Adaptation* (pp. 570-598). New York: Wiley.

Moffitt, T.E., Caspi, A., Dickson, N., Silva, P.A., & Stanton, W. (1996). Childhood-onset versus adolescent-onset antisocial conduct in males: Natural history from age 3 to 18. *Development and Psychopathology, 8,* 399-424.

Moffitt, T.E., & Caspi, A. (2001). Childhood predictors differentiate life-course persistent and adolescence-limited antisocial pathways, among males and females. *Development & Psychopathology, 13*, 355-375.

Moffitt, T.E., Caspi, A., Harrington, H., & Milne, B. (2002). Males on the life-course persistent and adolescence-limited antisocial pathways: Follow-up at age 26. *Development & Psychopathology, 14,* 179-206.

Monahan, K. C., Steinberg, L., Cauffman, E., & Mulvey, E. P. (2009). Trajectories of Antisocial Behavior and Psychosocial Maturity from Adolescence to Young Adulthood. *Developmental Psychology, 45*, 1654-1668.

Morenoff, J. D., Sampson, R. J., & Raudenbush, S. W. (2001). Neighborhood Inequality, collective efficacy, and the spatial dynamics of urban violence. *Criminology, 39,* 517-559.

Mulvey, E. P., Steinberg, L., Piquero, A. R., Besana, M., Fagan, J., Schubert, C. et al., (2010). Trajectories of desistance and continuity in antisocial behavior following court adjudication among serious adolescent offenders. *Development and Psychopathology, 22,* 453-475.

Nagelkerke, N.J. (1991). A note on a general definition of the coefficient of determination. *Biometrika, 78,* 691-692.

Nagin, D., & Farrington, D. (1992). The onset and persistence of offending. *Criminology, 30*, 501-525.

Nagin, D., & Tremblay, R. (1999). Trajectories of boys' physical aggression, opposition, and hyperactivity on the path to physically violent and non-violent delinquency. *Child Development, 70,* 1181-1196.

Overbeek, G., Stattin, H., Vermulst, A., Ha, T., Engels, R. (2007). Parent-child relationships, partner relationships, and emotional adjustment: A birth-to-maturity prospective study. *Developmental Psychology, 43,* 429-437.

Pagani, L.S., Japel, C., Vaillancourt, T., Tremblay, R.E., & Cote, S (2008). Links between the life course trajectories of family dysfunction and anxiety during middle childhood. *Journal of Abnormal Child Psychology, 36,* 41-53.

Patterson. G.R. (1995). Coercion as a basis for early age of onset for arrest. In J. McCord (Ed.), *Coercion and Punishment in Long-Term Perspective* (pp. 81-105). Cambridge, UK: Cambridge University Press.

Patterson, G.R., DeBaryshe, B.D., & Ramsey, E. (1989). A developmental perspective on antisocial behavior. *American Psychologist, 44,* 329-335.

Patterson, G., Reid, J., & Dishion, T. (1992). *Antisocial Boys.* Eugene, OR: Catalia.

Patterson, G. R., & Stouthamer-Loeber, M. (1984). The correlation of family management practices and delinquency. *Child Development, 55,* 1299 – 1307.

Peterson, L., Ewigman, B., & Kivlahan, C. (1993). Judgments regarding appropriate child supervision to prevent injury: The role of environmental risk and child age. *Child Development, 64,* 934-950.

Pettit, G. S., Bates, J. E., Dodge, K. A., & Meece, D. W. (1999). The impact of after-school peer contact on early adolescent externalizing problems is moderated by parental monitoring, perceived neighborhood safety, and prior adjustment. *Child Development, 70,* 768-778.

Preacher, K.J., & Hayes, A.F. (2004) SPSS and SAS procedures for estimating indirect effects in simple mediation models. *Behavior Research Methods, Instruments, & Computers, 36,* 717-731.

Raine, A. (1993). The Psychopathology of Crime: Criminal Behavior as a Clinical Disorder. San Diego, CA: Academic Press.

Raine, A., Moffitt, T.E., Caspi, A.C., Loeber, R., Stouthamer-Loeber, M., & Lynam, D. (2005). Neurocognitive impairments in boys on the life-course persistent antisocial path. *Journal of Abnormal Psychology, 114,* 38-49.

Rankin, B. H., & Quane, J.M. (2000). Neighborhood poverty and the social isolation of inner-city African American families. *Social Forces, 79,* 139–164.

Richter, J.E., & Martinez, P.E. (1993). The NIMH community violence project: I. Children as victims of and witnesses to violence. *Psychiatry, 56,* 7-21.

Rowe, D. (1994). The Limits of Family Influence: Genes, Experience, and Behavior. New York: Guildford Press.

Rutter, M.(1982). Prevention of children's psychosocial disorders: Myth and substance. *Pediatrics, 70,* 883.

Rutter, M., Giller, H., & Hagell, A. (1998). *Antisocial Behavior by Young People.* New York: Cambridge University Press.

Rutter, M. (1997). Nature-nurture integration: The example of antisocial behavior. *American Psychologist, 52,* 390-398.

Rutter, M., Silberg, J., O'Connor, T., & Simonoff, E. (1999). Genes and child psychiatry: Empirical research findings. *Journal of Child Psychology and Psychiatry, 40*, 19-55.

Rutter, M. (2003). Commentary: Causal processes leading to antisocial behavior. *Developmental Psychology, 39*, 372-378.

Sameroff, A. (2007). Identifying risk and protective factors for healthy child development. In A. Clarke-Stewart, & J. Dunn (Eds.), *Families Count*. New York: Cambridge University Press.

Sampson, R. (1992). Family management and child development: Insights from social disorganization theory. In J. McCord (Ed.), *Advances in Criminological Theory: Facts, Frameworks, and Forecasts*. New Brunswick: Transaction Press.

Sampson, R., & Groves, W. (1989). Community structure and crime: Testing social- disorganization theory. *American Journal of Sociology, 94,* 774-802.

Sampson, R.J., & Laub, J.H. (1990). Crime and deviance over the life course: The salience of adult social bonds. *American Sociological Review, 55,* 609-627.

Sampson, R.J., & Laub, J.H. (1993*). Crime in the Making: Pathways and Turning Points through Life*. Cambridge, MA: Harvard University Press.

Sampson, R.J., & Laub, J.H. (2003). Life-course desisters? Trajectories of crime among delinquent boys followed to age 70. *Criminology, 41,* 319-339.

Sampson, R.J., Morenoff, J., & Earls, F. (1999). Beyond social capital: Spatial dynamics of collective efficacy for children. *American Sociological Review, 64,* 633-660.

Sampson, R., Morenoff, J., & Gannon-Rowley, T. (2002). Assessing "neighborhood effects": Social processes and new directions in research. *Annual Review of Sociology, 28,* 443-478.

Sampson, R., Raudenbush, S., & Earls, F. (1997). Neighborhoods and violent crime: A multi level study of collective efficacy. *Science, 277,* 918-924.

Schaefer, J.L. (1997). *Analysis of Incomplete Multivariate Data.* London: Chapman & Hall.

Sears, R.R., Maccoby, E., & Levin, H. (1957). *Patterns of Childrearing.* Evanston, IL: Row, Peterson.

Sears, W., & Sears, M. (1995). *The Discipline Book.* Boston, MA: Little Brown & Company.

Shaw, D.S., Criss, M., Schonberg, M., & Beck, J. (2004). The development of family hierarchies and their relation to children's conduct problems. *Development and Psychopathology, 16,* 483-500

Sheidow. A.J., Gorman-Smith, D., Tolan, P.H., & Henry, D.B. (2001). Family and community characteristics: Risk factors for violence exposure in inner-city youth. *Journal of Community Psychology, 29,* 345-360.

Sheidow, A. J., Strachan, M. K., Minden, J. A., Henry, D. B., Tolan, P. H., & Gorman-Smith, D. (2008). The relation of antisocial behavior patterns and changes in internalizing symptoms for a sample of inner-city youth: Comorbidity within a developmental framework. *Journal of Youth and Adolescence, 37,* 821–829.

Simonoff, E., Elander, J., Holmshaw, J., Pickles, A., Murray, R., & Rutter, M. (2004). Predictors of antisocial personality: Continuities from childhood to adult life. *British Journal of Psychiatry, 184,* 118-127.

Simons, R., Simons, L., Burt, C., Brody, G., & Cutrona, C. (2005). Collective efficacy, authoritative parenting, and delinquency: A longitudinal test of a model integrating community- and family-level processes. *Criminology,* *43*, 989-1029.

Smith, J.R., Brooks-Gunn, J., & Klebanov, P.K. (1997). The consequences of living in poverty for young children's cognitive and verbal ability and early school achievement. In G.J. Duncan & J. Brooks-Gunn (Eds.). *Consequences of Growing Up Poor.* New York, NY: Russel Sage.

Spano, R., Vazsonyi, A.T., & Bolland, J. (2009). Does parenting mediate the effects of exposure to violence on violent behavior? An ecological-transactional model of community violence. *Journal of Adolescence, 32,* 1321-1341.

Spergel, I.A. (1990). Youth gangs: Continuity and change. In M. Tonry & N. Morris (Eds.), *Crime and Justice: A Review of the Literature* (pp. 171-275), Vol. 12. Chicago: The University of Chicago Press.

Sobel, M.E. (1982). Asymptotic intervals for indirect effects in structural equation models. In S. Leinhart (Ed.), *Sociological Methodology 1982* (pp. 290-312), San Francisco: Jossey- Bass.

Steinberg, L., Blatt- Eisengart, I., & Cauffman, E. (2006). Patterns of competence and adjustment among adolescents from authoritative, authoritarian, indulgent, and neglectful homes: A replication in a sample of serious juvenile offenders. *Journal of Research on Adolescence, 15,* 47-58.

Steinberg, L., & Morris, A.S. (2001). Adolescent development. *Annual Review of Psychology, 52,* 83-110.

Sterne, J., White, I., Carlin, J., Spratt, M., Royston, P., Kenward. M., Wood, A., & Carpenter, J. (2009).

Multiple imputation for missing data in epidemiological and clinical research: Potential and pitfalls. *British Medical Journal, 338*, b2393.

Stouthamer-Loeber, M., Loeber, R., Stallings, R., & Lacourse, E. (2008). Desistance from and persistence in offending. In R. Loeber, D. P. Farrington, M. Stouthamer-Loeber & H. R. White (Eds.), *Violence and Serious Theft: Risk and Promotive Factors from Childhood to Early Adulthood*. Mahwah, New Jersey: Lawrence Erlbaum.

Susman, E.J. (2006). Psychobiology of persistent antisocial behavior: Stress, early vulnerabilities and the attenuation hypothesis. *Neuroscience and Biobehavioral Reviews, 30,* 376-389.

Szapocznik, J., & Coatsworth, J.D. (1999). An ecodevelopmental framework for organizing the influences on drug abuse: A developmental model of risk and protection. In M. Glantz & C.R. Hartel (Eds.), *Drug Abuse: Origins and Interventions* (pp. 331-366). Washington, DC: American Psychological Association.

Thornberry, T.P., Huizinga, D., & Loeber, R. (1995). The prevention of serious delinquency and violence: Implications from the program of research on the causes and correlates of delinquency. In J.C. Howell, B. Krisbert, J.D. Hawkins, & J.J. Wilson (Eds.), *Sourcebook on Serious, Violent, and Chronic Juvenile Offenders* (pp. 213-237). Thousand Oaks, CA: Sage.

Tolan, P.H. (2009). *Developmental-Ecological Understanding of Relation of Delinquency to Adult Offending for Inner-City Males.* Powerpoint presented at Community Psychology Lunch of the University of Virginia, Charlottesville, VA.

Tolan, P.H., & Gorman-Smith, D. (1992). *Chicago Stress and Coping Interview Manual.* Chicago: Families and Communities Research Group, Institute for Juvenile Research, The University of Illinois at Chicago.

Tolan, P.H., & Gorman-Smith, D. (1993). *Chicago Youth Development Study Community Scales.* Chicago: Families and Communities Research Group, Institute for Juvenile Research, The University of Illinois at Chicago.

Tolan, P. H., Gorman-Smith, D., Huesmann, L.R., & Zelli, A. (1997). Assessment of family relationship characteristics: A measure to explain risk for antisocial behavior and depression in youth. *Psychological Assessment, 9,* 212-223.

Tolan, P.H., Gorman-Smith, D., & Henry, D.B. (2000). *Chicago Youth Development Study Parenting Practices Measure: Instructions for Scaling Technical Report.* Chicago: Families and Communities Research Group, Institute for Juvenile Research, The University of Illinois at Chicago.

Tolan, P.H., Gorman-Smith, D., & Henry, D.B. (2001a). *Chicago Youth Development Study Community and Neighborhood Measure: Construction and Reliability Technical Report.* Chicago: Families and Communities Research Group, Institute for Juvenile Research, The University of Illinois at Chicago.

Tolan, P.H., Gorman-Smith, D., & Henry, D.B. (2001b). *Chicago Youth Development Study Use of the Child Behavior Checklist: Technical Report.* Chicago: Families and Communities Research Group, Institute for Juvenile Research, The University of Illinois at Chicago.

Tolan, P.H., Gorman-Smith, D., & Henry, D.B. (2001c). *Chicago Youth Development Study Family Relationship Measure Scale Description.* Chicago: Families and Communities Research Group, Institute for Juvenile Research, The University of Illinois at Chicago.

Tolan, P.H., Gorman-Smith, D., & Henry, D.B. (2002). *Chicago Youth Development Study Self-Report Delinquency Scale Technical Report.* Chicago: Families and Communities Research Group, Institute for Juvenile Research, The University of Illinois at Chicago.

Tolan, P., Gorman-Smith, D., & Henry, D. (2003). The developmental ecology of urban males' youth violence. *Developmental Psychology, 39,* 274-291.

Tolan, P. H., Guerra, N. G., & Kendall, P. (1995). A developmental-ecological perspective on antisocial behavior in children and adolescents: Towards a unified risk and intervention framework. *Journal of Consulting and Clinical Psychology, 63,* 579-584.

Tolan, P.H., & Henry, D. (1996). Patterns of psychopathology among urban poor children: Comorbidity and aggression effects. *Journal of Consulting and Clinical Psychology, 64,* 1094-1099.

Tremblay, R.E., Nagin, D.S., Seguin, J.R., Zoccolillo, M., Zelazo, P.D., Boivin, M., et al. (2004). Physical aggression during early childhood: Trajectories and predictors. *Pediatrics, 114,* e43-e50.

Tremblay, R.E., Phil, R.O., Vitaro, F., & Dobkin, P.L. (1994). Predicting early onset of male AB from preschool behavior. *Archives of General Psychiatry, 51,* 732-739.

van Domburgh, L., Loeber, R., Bezemer, D., Stallings, R., & Stouthamer-Loeber, M. (2009). Childhood predictors of desistance and level of persistence in offending in early onset offenders. *Journal of Abnormal Child Psychology, 37,* 967-980.

Veenstra, R., Lindenberg, S., Verhulst, F.C., & Ormel, J. (2009). Childhood-limited versus persistent antisocial behavior: Why do some recover and others do not? The TRAILS study. *Journal of Early Adolescence, 29,* 718-742.

Wadsworth, M. E., & Compas, B. E. (2002). Coping with family and economic strain: The adolescent perspective. *Journal of Research on Adolescence, 12,* 243-274.

Wallen, J., & Rubin, R.H. (1997). The role of the family in mediating the effects of community violence on children. *Aggression and Violent Behavior, 2,* 33-41.

Wasserman, G.A., Miller, L.S., Pinner, M.A., & Jaramillo, B. (1996). Parenting predictors of early conduct problems in urban, high-risk boys. *Journal of the American Academy of Child & Adolescent Psychiatry, 35,* 1227-1236.

Webster-Stratton, C. (1998). Parent training with low-income clients: Promoting parental engagement through a collaborative approach. In J.R. Lutzker (Ed.), *Child Abuse: A Handbook of Theory, Research and Treatment* (pp. 183-210). New York, NY: Plenum Press.

Wikstrom, P.H., & Loeber, R. (1999). Do Disadvantaged Neighborhoods Cause Well-adjusted Children to Become Adolescent Delinquents?: A Study of Male Juvenile Serious Offending, Individual Risk and Protective Factors, and Neighborhood Context. Western

Psychiatric Institute, School of Medicine, University of Pittsburgh.

Wilson, W.J. (1987). The Truly Disadvantaged: The Inner City, the Underclass, and Public Policy. Chicago: University of Chicago Press.

Wilson, W.J. (1996). *When Work Disappears*. New York: Knopf

Index

9 781593 327149